The Aga khan Delusion

A Tale of Sex, Lies and Deception

Salim Lalani

Copyright

ISBN:978-1-7640148-0-9

Title: The Aga Khan Delusion: A Tale of Sex, Lies and
Deception

Genre: Non-fiction

Author: Salim Lalani

Email: salim@calltowakeup.org.au

Website: https://calltowakeup.org.au

Disclaimer

This book contains an overview of Islamic history, drawing upon diverse sources and interpretations. The content reflects a range of perspectives on historical events, figures and developments. It is important to note that Islamic history, like any other historical subject, is subject to various interpretations, and views may differ among scholars, practitioners and communities.

While every effort has been made to ensure accuracy, the author acknowledges that historical narratives can be complex and evolving. The information presented in this book does not claim to represent the views of any specific school of thought or tradition within Islam, nor does it intend to offend or misrepresent any group or belief.

Readers are encouraged to approach the material with an open mind and seek further study from multiple sources to gain a comprehensive understanding of the topic. The author assumes no responsibility for the interpretation or application of the material discussed in this book.

It is easier to believe in a fantasy you've heard a thousand times than to believe the truth for the first time.

Note

Throughout this work, owing to evolution of Shia Islam, particularly the Ismaili sect, the followers of Aga khan have been referred to as Ismailis, Nizari Ismailis, and Agakhanis.

Dedication

Dedicated to my parents, Late Mr. Fida Hussain Lalani, and Mrs. Amina Lalani for their unwavering love and dedication to my wellbeing.

Foreword

Throughout history, religious and dynastic narratives have been shaped by those in power, often leaving behind a trail of unanswered questions and suppressed voices.

In this thought-provoking volume, Lalani takes on the formidable task of peeling back the layers of history, tradition, and leadership within the Aga khan community.

His meticulous research and candid revelations provide readers with an unfiltered look into the evolution of Agakhanism, the making of the Aga Khan dynasty, and the intricate web of beliefs that have defined this faith over centuries.

Lalani's work is not merely an academic pursuit, but it is a deeply personal journey. Having spent decades as a devoted Agakhani, he understands the frustrations, dilemmas, and silent inquiries that many within the community grapple with.

His exploration into the origins of Agakhanism, the conversion of Hindus in the subcontinent, and the controversies surrounding its leadership is both bold and illuminating.

With over two hundred videos on YouTube, Lalani has become a voice for those who dare to question, a chronicler of history that many may not have encountered before.

The fact that his findings have resonated with hundreds of thousands worldwide speaks volumes about the hunger for knowledge and the courage required to seek it.

His work is not without resistance—true exploration rarely is—but his persistence is a testament to his commitment to truth.

This book is more than just a historical account; it is an invitation to reflect, to question, and to understand the evolution of Agakhanism in its entirety.

Whether you are an Agakhani seeking deeper insight, a historian eager to explore lesser-known narratives, or simply a curious reader, this volume will challenge, enlighten, and engage you.

Lalani's dedication to this subject, despite the obstacles he faces, is commendable. I hope that his work continues to inspire thoughtful discourse.

Sultan Bhatia

An Agakhani

Table of Contents

Introduction **12**

Book One... **28**

    Islam and Ismailism.................................. 28

Chapter One...................................... **29**

    The Prophet and Mawla Ali.......................... 29

Chapter 2... **40**

    Ismailism 40

Chapter 3... **62**

    Nizari Ismailism 62

Book 2 .... **80**

    Divorcing Islam.................................. 80

Chapter One...................................... **81**

    Mission India.................................... 81

    The Aga Khan....................................109

Chapter 3...**133**

    Aga Khan III – A Political Genius 133

Chapter 4...**223**

    Adventures of Prince Alykhan.................... 223

Book 3 ....**240**

    Beginning of An End.............................240

Chapter One: K **241**

Chapter 2...**274**

    Spiritual Deception 274

    The Spiritual Franchise.........................292

Chapter Four.....................................**309**

Islamic Conscience 309

Chapter Five..**318**

The Political Clout..318

Chapter Six...**330**

The Common Man...330

Introduction

It has been more than fifty-five years.

I don't recall the exact year or date, but the memory of Karimabad *Jamaatkhana* (a place of Aga Khan worship) in South Mumbai remains vivid. I was nine years old, standing on the second floor of the building, surrounded by thousands of people who had gathered there. The air crackled with anticipation, an almost tangible energy flowing through the crowd.

We were waiting for a moment beyond ordinary experience to meet our Lord and Master, Hazar Imam, Shah Karim, Aga Khan IV.

All around me, tears of reverence glistened on countless cheeks. The air was thick with the heady aroma of incense, and a chorus of *ginans* (devotional hymns) swelled through the hall. The local missionaries, their voices rich with religious fervor, and unshakable conviction, entranced the *Jamaat* (congregation) preparing them to bask in the *Noor* (the divine light) of the celestial being, their Imam, Aga khan IV.

Then, after what felt like an eternity, the wail of police sirens shattered the hush, heralding the lord's arrival.

Time stopped and hearts pounded in unison!

It wasn't long before a figure dressed in angelic white, his skin just as luminous, entered the hall. Sunlight streamed through the windows, amplifying his ethereal glow. A thousand-strong chorus began reciting the *salwat* (a prayer) in hushed reverence:

Allahumma salli 'ala Muhammadin wa 'ala ali Muhammad.

meaning

O Allah, send peace upon Muhammad and his progeny (Aga khan)

The lord stepped onto a red carpet, which was laid in a deliberate zigzag fashion across the hall so that every disciple could bask in the radiance of his presence.

They could not get enough.

After all, God himself was before them, in flesh and blood.

The path led him to a chair on the stage, one that resembled a throne. He sank into it, flanked by kneeling officials awaiting his command.

A *ginan* followed, its haunting melody pleading the divine being for protection and well-being of the *Jamaat*. Then, the lord rose to deliver the *farman* (a religious edict). As always, it began with spiritual blessings, followed by words of guidance, advice on both spiritual and worldly affairs, reassurances that his love for his followers surpassed their love for him and that even after he departed from *Jamaat Khana,* they would remain in his heart.

Finally, he closed with more blessings.

The *farman* lasted only minutes. Once finished, he resumed his place on the throne as another voice translated his words into the local vernacular… English being beyond the reach of most devotees in those days.

A few ceremonies followed, and then he was gone.

His departure, however, cracked open the emotional floodgates. I remember people sobbing openly, embracing one another, and exchanging congratulations.

Why wouldn't they?

It is believed that just laying eyes on Aga khan washes away all sins!!

Once he had left, we were all as pure as the driven snow. But none of us, not the weeping devotees, not the elated congregation, and certainly not me knew the truth.

The divine being who had just blessed and purified us was a sinner himself.

From an Islamic perspective, an Imam leads prayers in a mosque, for Shia Muslims, he is a divine guide but for followers of Aga Khan, he is God himself in human form.

I was born into the Aga Khan cult, indoctrinated from an early age to believe that Aga Khan was God personified. He owned me, my soul and, more importantly, my wealth. My life's purpose, I was taught, was to serve him and his community.

With years of relentless conditioning, it was no surprise that I grew into a staunch believer, dedicating decades of my life to his commune in various capacities. It was only in the twilight of my life that a personal crisis cast the first ray of light on the truth.

Like every devotee, I believed that God had manifested in the person of Aga Khan as *Mushkil kusha* (the remover of difficulties), But that belief began to waver in 2011 when I found myself trapped in a crippling crisis. It was during this period of distress that a sermon delivered by the late Abu Ali, a well-known Aga Khan missionary, flashed through my mind.

He had once told a story of an Aga Khan devotee suffering a severe financial setback. Desperate for relief, the man sought guidance from the missionary who, in his wisdom, asked if the man had been paying *dasond,* the mandatory 12.5% religious tax to Aga Khan.

It was like asking a man dying of thirst if he had water!

The missionary continued: he had advised the man to pay *dasond* consistently for three months, boldly declaring that if his financial troubles did not vanish, he could spit in his face. The sermon, however, did not reveal if the advice had worked.

Was it truly that simple? I thought.

Could paying *dasond* redeem us from all difficulties? If so, why was I struggling? I had been paying *dasond* my entire life, through thick and thin.

Desperate for answers, I reached out to a missionary I knew in India. He assured me that *dasond* was as essential as food. Just as food nourishes the body, *dasond* sustains the soul. To reinforce his argument, he shared a story.

Once, Aga Khan III, the 48th Nizari Shia Imam, held a *darbar* (public audience) for his spiritual children in India. Among the congregation was an elderly woman, a devoted follower. She was eager to know whether she would achieve salvation upon her death. When her turn came, she presented *mehmani* (gifts) to the Imam and asked the burning question.

The Imam assured her that she was an elevated soul—so much so that in a past life, she had died for Imam Husayn, his alleged ancestor. Overcome with confusion, she asked, if that were true, why was she still trapped in the endless cycle of birth and death?

Imam's response?

Because she had failed to pay *dasond* in her past life!!

The story did not bring me relief, rather it deepened my doubt!!

To the revered Imam, *dasond* was the key to salvation, not the ultimate sacrifice of one's life!!

And yet, my question remained unanswered.

Why was I still suffering when I had paid dasond my entire life?

From that moment on, I practiced observation.

When in *Jamaatkhana* I began observing my actions. Soon, I realized they were devoid of understanding, my participation in rituals was mechanical and my awareness was empty. This practice led to awareness which ultimately revealed the truth.

I was a victim of fraud!

Yet, what recourse does one have as a devotee of Aga Khan?

After all, the basic human rights of freedom to speak and express oneself, are denied by the system. To question Aga Khan, his system, or even his leaders, is a taboo. It invites severe consequences such as ostracism, excommunication, and disgrace.

Had one ever dared to speak out, they would not have been the only one to suffer, their family, too, would have been condemned.

That is the Aga khan version of Pluralism inside the *Jamatkhana*!!

Naturally, I chose silence. But fate had other plans. Three years later, an incident shattered my restraint.

Among Aga Khan devotees, religious gatherings called *majlises* play a significant role in so-called spiritual practice. One such gathering, *Fidai*, is no ordinary *majalis*. It is secretive, exclusive, and ironically the spiritual meeting is only accessible through an exorbitant membership fee.

Like any other *majlis, Fidai* gathering is conducted by *Mukhi,* (Aga Khan's appointed representative) in *Jamatkhanas* across the globe. In 2014, I was appointed *Mukhi* of *Fidai majlis* in Sydney. Before assuming my role, I, like all new *Mukhis,* had to undergo an induction session to familiarize myself with the protocols, rights, and obligations of the position.

It was during this induction that a single question and its unsettling answer changed the course of my life. The question came from a *Mukhiani* (*Mukhi's* wife) and it concerned a protocol.

Unbelievable as it may seem, many Aga Khan devotees wish for their deceased family members to be enrolled in the *Fidai majlis*. It is believed its spiritual powers would ultimately liberate their souls.

The *Mukhiani* understood that as part of the protocol, followers seeking admission to *Fidai*, needed to pay a membership fee, take an oath of secrecy, and pledge to sacrifice their life when required.

But she was unclear about the protocol to admit deceased devotees!!

Upon asking the question, Mr. Malik Lalani (no relation to me), the instructor of the induction, responded without hesitation:

"The protocol remains the same as that for a living person."

This meant that even a deceased person had to pay the membership fee, take an oath of secrecy, and pledge to sacrifice their life when…. They are already dead!!

The *Mukhiani* seemed satisfied with this response, but I was stunned.

Mr. Lalani's response defied logic.

As *Mukhi,* the Commander of the army, I was happy to lead soldiers to a mission but was not too sure about taking the dead ones along!!

I needed clarification.

During the refreshment break, I took Mr. Lalani aside and voiced my concern. To my surprise, he looked just as baffled as I was. Either he did not understand the role of a *Fidai,* or he was aware of the folly and had hoped it would never come to light.

An awkward silence stretched between us.

When he realized that he was cornered, he did what the Aga Khan's leaders typically do in such situations. He began slithering away, hoping to evade further questioning. This was the unspoken signal that I had crossed a line. Logical, intelligent questions that challenge the system's tenets are unwelcome.

But I was relentless. I stopped his flow and insisted on an answer. Reluctantly, he promised to seek clarification from his superiors.

Five weeks passed.

When he finally called, my initial excitement quickly turned to disbelief!!

"The Imam has allowed deceased members to be admitted to Fidai," he said matter-of-factly.

According to this decree, the dead could become soldiers, and I would be responsible for leading them on missions when required!!

Every syllable of Mr. Lalani's response lacked logic but importantly it reeked of authoritarianism. The message was clear:

I was to obey without question.

For me, that was the last straw!

As an Aga khan follower, to that point, I had been a devout follower. I had fulfilled my religious duties, served the Aga Khan and his community, and paid my religious dues…even during financial hardship.

Yet, for all my unwavering allegiance, reverence, service, and financial tributes, I could not even receive a sensible answer to a simple question…let alone the promised heaven in this world and the next!!

On June 29, 2014, I retracted my oath of allegiance to Aga Khan.

With my belief system shattered, I instinctively embarked on a journey to seek my spiritual path. At the time, I had no intention of speaking out against the system. But a few months later, an incident changed everything.

An Aga khan follower, a friend reached out to me, desperate for help. His family was facing a financial crisis severe enough to tear them apart. We met in my office to discuss solutions. It soon became clear that his troubles were deeply rooted in his belief system.

Like every devout follower, he had been paying 12.5% of his income as a mandatory religious tax (*dasond*) to Aga khan, along with an array of other religious dues.

Yet, in his time of dire need, the system had turned cold shoulder.

The problem was easy to identify, and the solution was equally clear. However, saying it out loud had consequences. After all, like all devotees, he had been indoctrinated since childhood. His ability to reason had been systematically eroded. He firmly believed that paying the Aga Khan was essential for his salvation. The fear had been ingrained in him that failure to give *dasond* would condemn him to hell in the afterlife.

It was ironic that he didn't realize that he and his family were in hell here and now - all to avoid an imaginary one in the hereafter!!

But I had a dilemma on my hands.

If I told him the truth, I would lose him as a friend and if I refrained, his suffering would continue.

After a moment of contemplation, I gathered courage and asked,

"How necessary is it to share your already modest income with your Imam when your family needs it to survive?"

As expected, he stared at me in shock. Then, without a word, he abruptly stood up, walked to the door, turned back, and said,

"I will die. My family will die. But I will not stop paying my Imam."

With that, he slammed the door behind him.

After he had left, I sank into my chair, overwhelmed by the sheer power of human irrationality. A barrage of questions flooded my mind.

How could a man live in suffering here just to avoid imaginary suffering in the afterlife? Who or what had stripped him of his ability to reason? If this was happening in a first-world country like Australia, what about the millions in the third world?

On that spring day of 2014, I made a resolution.

I would dedicate the rest of my life to creating awareness.

This work is but a small step toward that mission. It aims to create awareness about the Aga Khan construct, to expose his spiritual and humanitarian sham and to encourage his followers to think for themselves rather than be controlled.

It also seeks to shed light on the criminal aspects of the Aga Khan system so that public and private institutions reconsider funding his so-called humanitarian activities.

Furthermore, this book seeks to alert the global Muslim community to the blatant acts of Islamic blasphemy that occur in *Jamaatkhanas* worldwide.

Since its inception in the eighth century, the history of Aga Khan's alleged ancestors has been shrouded in mystery. For over 1,250 years, they lived and died in secret, paranoid underground environments. Hiding behind this historical fog, the Aga Khan IV established an Ismaili Constitution in 1986, claiming direct descent from the

Prophet Muhammad through his daughter Fatima and the first Shia Imam, Ali ibn Abi Talib.

"Mawlana Hazar Imam Shah Karim al Hussaini, His Highness Prince Aga Khan, in direct lineal descent from the Holy Prophet (s.a.s.) through Hazrat Mawlana Ali (a.s.) through Hazrat Bibi Fatima (a.s.), is the Forty-Ninth Imam of the Ismaili Muslims."

The Preamble of the Shia Imami Ismaili Constitution

--

The declaration, h o w e v e r , conflicts with tenets of Ismaili Muslims outside of Aga khan fold and the holy Quran.

We shall elaborate upon these in later chapters.

It is, however, clear from Islamic perspective that Aga khan could not have descended from the Prophet. After all, Islam does not recognize descent via a female issue and the Prophet's sons did not survive to further his progeny.

But the question remains…is Aga khan a descendant of *Mawla Ali* and hence a legitimate Shia Imam?

To find the answer, we must begin our journey in seventh-century Arabia tracking through history to arrive in modern-day Europe where the Aga Khan IV died on 4th February 2025.

Book One

Islam and Ismailism

Chapter One

The Prophet and Mawla Ali

P re-Islamic Arabia was a land of nomadic tribes, where society was predominantly male-dominated, and religious practices ranged from the monotheistic traditions of the Abrahamic faiths to the polytheistic beliefs of Arab pagans.

Around 1,400 years ago, this arid land captured the world's attention.

On 8 June 570 CE, Amyna bint Wahhab, a widow from the Quraysh tribe, gave birth to a son in Mecca. This child would be known to the world as Mohammad, the Prophet of Islam.

The world would never be the same again!

True to tradition, the infant Mohammad spent the early years of his life in the open desert, cared for by a wet nurse named Halima. At the age of six, he returned to Mecca, only to face a tragedy: his mother, Amyna, passed away, leaving him an orphan. His father, Abdullah, had already died during Amyna's pregnancy.

As a boy, Mohammad tended sheep and, as he grew older, entered trade. Eventually, he became a business agent for a successful merchant, a forty-year-old widow named Khadija, whom he married when he was twenty-five.

Prophethood

The cave of Hira, located about fourteen kilometers from present-day Mecca, holds a pivotal place in Islamic history. It is here that the journey of Islam began. Mohammad regularly visited the cave to meditate and reflect.

One fateful day it is believed, while in deep contemplation, the angel Gabriel appeared to him, instructing him to read from a tablet. Being an Ummi, (illiterate) Mohammad was unable to read.

He responded, *"I cannot read."*

The angel, however, insisted and urged him again. After three attempts, it is said that Mohammad could miraculously read the following words:

Proclaim! (or read!) in the name of thy Lord and Cherisher, who created man out of a (mere) clot of congealed blood. Proclaim! And thy Lord is Most Bountiful

Who taught (the use of) the pen, taught man that which he knew not

Sura 96, Al-Alaq, Ayat 1-5

This revelation marked the beginning of Islam as a religion and Mohammad as its prophet. It also inaugurated a tradition of divine revelations that continued until the prophet's passing. These revelations were later compiled into what is now known as the Holy Quran, the Islamic scripture.

The first to accept the new faith were the Prophet's wife, Khadija, his cousin, Ali, the servant of his household, Zayd ibn Harithah, his close friend, Abu Bakr, and several members of his extended family. They embraced Islam by reciting the Shahada, the declaration of faith:

"There is no God but Allah, and Muhammad is the messenger of Allah."

Persecution and Migration

Pre-Islamic Mecca was primarily a polytheistic society, though it also hosted communities of Jews, Zoroastrians, and Christians. The Prophet's message of Islam came as a revolutionary force that shook the very foundations of pre-Islamic belief systems. It challenged ancestral customs and disrupted a deeply entrenched social and economic order. Unsurprisingly, the Prophet's proclamation was seen as blasphemous, outrageous, and offensive.

Meccans had to address the problem the Prophet had presented.

Initially, they ridiculed and dismissed the Prophet as a madman. But when the Prophet did not relent, persecution, social boycotts, torture, and killings followed. For the next twelve years, the Prophet and his small group of followers endured ongoing hostility.

Eventually, facing mounting oppression, the Prophet considered migration, not only as an escape from persecution but to find support for his monotheistic message.

Relief came when the people of Yathrib, an oasis town to the north of Mecca, reached out with messages of support and invited Muslims to migrate.

The Prophet accepted the invitation and set off towards Yathrib.

This event, known as the Hijra (migration), marks year one of the Islamic calendar, which corresponds to 622 CE in the Gregorian calendar.

Despite several attempts by the Meccans to arrest him, the Prophet safely reached Yathrib, where he was given a warm welcome.

From that moment, the town became known *as Al-Madina al-Munawwara,* or the *"Illuminated City."*

Today, it is known as Medina.

The people of Medina, called the *Ansars* (helpers), warmly welcomed the migrants, known as *Muhajirun,* and assisted with their resettlement. The Prophet established a unique bond of brotherhood between each *Ansar* and *Muhajir*, ensuring that the former, regardless of their economic status, supported the latter. Charitable giving was formalized, and *zakat* (charity) became one of the Five Pillars of Islam.

One of the Prophet's primary tasks upon arriving in Medina was to lay the foundation for the first mosque, Masjid al-Nabawi. Over time, it became a center for both worship and governance.

A covenant was established to ensure harmonious relationships with people of different faiths, and the concept of common citizenship was introduced, outlining the principles for regulating the town's affairs.

Ali ibn Abu Talib

Ali ibn Abu Talib, born in 600 CE to Abu Talib ibn Abd al-Muttalib and Fatima bint Asad, was the Prophet's first cousin. Since their respective fathers, Abu Talib and Abdullah were brothers, Ali and the Prophet shared a close familial bond. Ali's connection to the Prophet ran deeper than blood when he married Fatima, the Prophet's daughter.

The Prophet raised Ali as a son and even named him. However, Ali's mother, Fatima, called him Haydar, the Lion. He is also known by several honorific titles, including al-Murtada (the one with whom God is pleased), Asad Allah (the Lion of God), and Amir al-Mu'minin (Commander of the Faithful).

At just ten years old, Ali was one of the first male to accept the Prophet's message and supported him without hesitation. Throughout the years, he played a pivotal role in both the battlefield and the mosque, establishing Islam's presence.

Ali is revered to this day for his courage, integrity, and unwavering dedication to Islam. Given his significant contributions, Ali is regarded as second only to the Prophet in importance in the Islamic world.

Ghadir-e-Khumm

In 631 CE, the Prophet left Medina to perform the *Hajj*, an annual pilgrimage to Mecca. Accompanied by 100,000 Muslims, it was to be his final pilgrimage.

On his return journey, roughly 64 kilometers north of Mecca, at a location known as *Ghadir-e-Khumm*, the Prophet received a divine revelation, which was more of an ultimatum.

O Messenger! Deliver what has been revealed to you from your Lord; and if you do it not, then you have not delivered His message, and Allah will protect you from the people; surely Allah will not guide the unbelieving people."

Surah al-Ma`idah: Ayat 5:67

The Prophet, for some reason, had been postponing the delivery of a previous command which, as many believe was essential to define the religion of Islam.

On this day, however, the Prophet had no choice but to deliver it. He halted the caravan, summoning those ahead and waiting for those behind. Once all had gathered, he was elevated on a platform so that everyone could see him. The Prophet then delivered a *Khutba* (sermon)

In a nutshell, the sermon stressed the significance of maintaining unity and brotherhood within the Muslim community after he had passed.

Regarding his succession, he designated Ali as *Mawla* (master), highlighting his deep understanding of Islam and urged Muslims to follow his example.

Then, taking Ali by the hand, he addressed the crowd:

Am I not your *Mawla*?

After receiving affirmation, the Prophet declared:

He whose *Mawla* I am, Ali is his *Mawla*.

Umar ibn al-Khattab, a close companion of the Prophet, congratulated Ali, saying, "You have now become the *Mawla* of every faithful man and woman."

From that moment, Ali became known as Mawla Ali, the master of the faithful.

The caravan then resumed its journey to Medina, unaware that the Prophet's declaration, particularly the appointment of Ali as *Mawla,* would give rise to a schism that would forever change the course of Islamic history and the world order.

The Prophet's Death and Division of Islam

During the twenty-two years of his prophethood, the Prophet firmly established Islam, preached the Oneness of God, and conveyed divine revelations to his followers. However, two months after the event at Ghadir-e-Khumm, the Prophet fell ill.

On 8 June 632 CE, he led the morning prayers and, after returning home, passed away in the arms of Aisha, his beloved wife.

His final words were:

'O Allah, (with) the higher companions'

As the Prophet's body was being prepared for burial, a group of Muslims gathered at a place called the Saqifa to discuss the urgent question of succession. Although the Prophet had declared Ali as *Mawla*, for most, that did not mean he would succeed the Prophet.

The dilemma was profound!

Who could succeed the Prophet, given that the Holy Quran had declared him the *Khatam al-Anbiya* (Seal of the Prophets)?

After a heated debate, Abu Bakr, the Prophet's friend, and father-in-law, was elected to succeed. Not as a Prophet, but as a Caliph who would administer the Islamic state.

To the Muslims, the Holy Quran and the Prophet's *Sunna,* (legacy) were adequate to guide them on the right path.

However, not all agreed!!

A faction led by influential figures like Salman al-Farsi, Abu Dharr al-Ghiffari, and Ammar ibn Yasir argued that Mawla Ali, the Prophet's nominated successor should assume leadership. Despite their objections, Mawla Ali accepted the election of Abu Bakr. He gracefully refrained from open rebellion and chose to maintain unity within the Muslim community.

However, the controversy over his rightful position would soon evolve into a theological and political divide.

Abu Bakr's followers came to be known as Sunni Muslims as they were content with Prophet's Sunna as a source of divine guidance. On the other hand, Mawla Ali's supporters maintained he had the right qualifications to guide the Ummah. This party became known as Shi'atu Ali (the party of Ali) or Shia Muslims.

Thus, Muslims had been split between Sunnis and Shias…. when the incense on the Prophet's grave was still burning!!

Chapter 2

Ismailism

The Rashidun Caliphate

After Mawla Ali withdrew from the leadership contest, Abu Bakr, was appointed as the first Caliph to lead the Muslim community. His appointment marked the beginning of the Rashidun (Rightly Guided) Caliphate, which saw four Caliphs at its helm: Abu Bakr ibn Quhafa, Umar ibn al-Khattab, Uthman ibn Affan, and, finally, Shia Imam Mawla Ali ibn Abu Talib.

Despite the establishment of many Caliphates throughout Islamic history, none were considered "rightly guided" after the Rashidun period.

Notably, after the assassination of the third Caliph, Uthman, Mawla Ali was elected as Caliph by both Shia and Sunni Muslims. Thus, Mawla Ali, a member of the Ahl al-Bayt (the Prophet's family), finally assumed the Caliphate in 656 CE.... twenty-four years after the Prophet had designated him as Mawla at Ghadir e Khumm.

However, Mawla Ali's rise to the Caliphate was hardly a bed of roses!!

One of his first acts as Caliph was to dismiss Caliph Uthman's corrupt governors and redistribute *zakat* revenues according to divine instruction. This decision was unpopular among some factions, leading to escalating opposition. Besides, Mawla Ali's status and position also bred envy.

After all, he was a member of the Prophet's family (Ahl al-Bayt), a revered Shia Imam, a celebrated military hero, and now the Islamic Caliph. It was no surprise that he had numerous enemies.

Among those discontented were the followers of the slain Uthman. They suspected Mawla Ali as the architect of his murder and harbored a deep resentment and thirsted for retribution. Mawla Ali was aware of these sentiments but remained oblivious to an unlikely adversary, Aisha, the Prophet's widow.

Aisha's animosity towards Mawla Ali stemmed from a deep personal history. At one point, Mawla Ali had suggested to the Prophet to divorce Aisha following rumors of an extramarital affair. Though the allegations were never proven, the suggestion strained the relationship between Mawla Ali and Aisha, sowing the seeds of hostility that would later contribute to the political and military conflicts of the period.

Aisha's resentment towards Mawla Ali reached its peak following the assassination of Uthman, which presented her with an opportunity to settle old scores. Aisha accused him of orchestrating Uthman's murder and, in December 656 CE, declared war.

The conflict came to be known as the Battle of the Camel, named after the red camel Aisha rode into battle. Despite her resolve, Aisha was defeated and sent back to Hejaz, where she retired from politics.

However, Mawla Ali's troubles were far from over. Just as Aisha had opposed him, Muawiya ibn Abu Sufyan, the governor of Syria, harbored ambitions of overthrowing Mawla Ali's Caliphate.

In 657 CE, Muawiya sent a letter to the Syrian shura (council), accusing Mawla Ali of Uthman's murder and declaring war. The ensuing battle, known as the Battle of Siffin, took place on the banks of the Euphrates River, in what is now modern-day Iraq.

On the third day of the battle, Mawla Ali's forces had the upper hand, but Muawiya's army employed a clever tactic to avoid total defeat. They raised copies of the Holy Quran on their lances, calling for arbitration. Reluctantly, Mawla Ali agreed to cease fighting.

A faction within his ranks vehemently rejected the arbitration proposal as they could see through the enemy plot. These rejecters later became known as Kharjites or the Rejecters.

Despite the opposition, Mawla Ali remained firm, opting for arbitration which ultimately turned against him. In 659 CE, the arbitrators deposed him, and Muawiya claimed the Caliphate. Meanwhile, the Kharijites, dissatisfied with Mawla Ali's actions, would later rebel against him and his descendants.

With Muawiya's rise to power, Mawla Ali lost considerable support both from his army and the broader Muslim community. He eventually withdrew from political life, focusing on his role as a spiritual leader until his death.

On 28 January 661 CE, while offering the morning prayers in a mosque in Kufa, Mawla Ali was struck on the head with a poison-coated sword by a Kharijite named Abd al-Rahman ibn Muljam al-Muradi. Two days later, he succumbed to his injuries.

He was laid to rest in Najaf, Iraq, where his shrine stands as a site of reverence to this day.

He was sixty-two.

Legacy

Mawla Ali will always be remembered for his unparalleled courage, heroism, and unwavering devotion to the Islamic cause. Sunni Muslims honor him as a Rashidun Caliph, while Shia Muslims revere him as their first Imam, an inspiration for the institution of *Imamah,* which they believe, serves as the source of divine guidance.

His death marked the loss of a towering figure in Islamic history and the end of the Rashidun Caliphate.

The Battle of Karbala

Mawla Ali's passing brought about profound political changes. One of them was the rise of the Umayyad Caliphate under the leadership of Muawiya ibn Abu Sufyan. Meanwhile, Shia Muslims recognized Mawla Ali's eldest son, Hassan ibn Ali, as the next Shia Imam.

But Imam Hassan, to the dismay of Caliph Muawiya, claimed Islamic Caliphate as his right. After all, he was the grandson of the prophet and successor of the last Rashidun Caliph, Mawla Ali.

It was hardly a surprise that the mighty Caliph decided to confront Imam Hassan.

Recognizing that he was no match for Muawiya's military strength, Imam Hassan faced growing internal unrest within his ranks. A mutiny broke out in his camp, further demoralizing the army. With no feasible option left, Imam Hassan was forced to seek a peaceful resolution.

Muawiya suggested that Imam Hassan abdicate his claim to the Caliphate. In exchange, Muawiya promised him succession to the Caliphate after him. Left with little choice, Imam Hassan agreed, and a treaty was signed, which came to be known as the Hassan-Muawiya Treaty.

With Imam Hassan out of the political equation, Caliph Muawiya founded the Umayyad Caliphate, named after the Umayya tribe to which he belonged.

Now that he had secured the throne, Muawiya publicly renounced the terms of the Hassan-Muawiya treaty. Instead, he nominated his son, Yazid, as the next Caliph thus cementing the dynastic nature of the Umayyad rule.

Imam Hassan, on the other hand, had no choice but to retire from political life. He settled in Medina, where he tragically succumbed to poisoning on 2 April 670 CE.

His untimely death cast a shadow of suspicion, with many pointing the finger at Caliph Muawiya as the mastermind behind the assassination.

After the death of Imam Hassan, his younger brother, Husayn ibn Ali, a prominent Islamic figure, ascended as the third Imam of Shia Muslims. However, his rise raised a significant question:

Would he lay claim to the Caliphate, as his brother had?

This question weighed heavily on the mind of Yazid, the nascent Umayyad Caliph. To preempt any challenge to his rule, Yazid demanded that Imam Husayn pledge allegiance to him—a demand that was vehemently declined.

Meanwhile, the people of Kufa, a Shia stronghold, rallied behind Imam Husayn. They pledged their loyalty and urged him to claim his rightful position as Caliph, offering military support to overthrow Yazid.

Although Imam Husayn accepted the call, he sought confirmation of the loyalty of the people of Kufa. He sent his cousin, Muslim ibn Aqil, to gauge the situation. Once Muslim confirmed the support, Imam Husayn left Mecca for Kufa, accompanied by fifty members of his family, including women and children.

But tides had shifted since he began the fateful journey!!

Yazid, informed of Imam Husayn's plans, appointed Ubaidullah ibn Ziyad as the governor of Kufa. He swiftly intimidated Imam's supporters, forcing them to retract their support. Furthermore, to cement his control, he had Muslim ibn Aqil executed.

When Imam Husayn received the word of his cousin's death, he was already enroute to Kufa. Despite the grim news, the Imam chose to continue his journey, dismissing calls to return to Mecca.

The revered Imam and his party were now marching towards their death!!

On 2 October 680 CE, Imam Husayn and his party arrived at Karbala, a desolate plain located seventy kilometers north of Kufa, along the banks of the Euphrates River. Upon hearing of their arrival, Yazid dispatched an army of 4,000 men under the command of Umar ibn Sa'ad.

Umar demanded that Imam Husayn submit and pay his allegiance to Yazid.

Imam Husayn refused!!

In a brutal move to force submission, Umar's forces blocked access to the Euphrates River, cutting off the Imam's party from water. Facing death by either sword or thirst, Imam Husayn advised his followers to flee before the situation worsened.

Yet, his party chose death over deserting their Imam.

As a result, seventy-two of Imam Husayn's companions, including women and children, were martyred. Only Imam Husayn's eldest son, Ali al-Sajjad, survived, as he was unable to fight due to illness. Imam Husayn himself endured more than sixty wounds, was trampled by horses, and was ultimately beheaded.

Though Shia Islam had been born with the Prophet's passing, it was the martyrdom of Imam Husayn that solidified the Shia identity. Every year, Shia Muslims commemorate the Battle of Karbala over ten days in the Islamic month of Muharram, culminating on the tenth day known as *Ashura*.

Birth of Ismailism

After Imam Husayn's tragic death, his son, Ali al-Sajjad (also known as Zain ul-Abidin), became the fourth

Shia Imam. Due to the volatile political climate and the ongoing persecution by the Umayyads, he led a quiet life in Medina. Despite his efforts to maintain peace, his enemies eventually poisoned him to death in 713 CE.

His son, Muhammad Baqir, succeeded him as the fifth Imam. Like his father, Imam Baqir met the same tragic fate when he was poisoned to death in 732 CE, after guiding the Shia community for two decades. The deceased Imam's eldest son, Jafar ibn Muhammad al-Sadiq, became the sixth Imam of Shia Muslims.

Imam Jafar was a towering figure in Islamic history, revered by both Shia and Sunni Muslims. As an Islamic scholar, jurist, and theologian, he made lasting contributions, particularly as the founder of the Ja'fari school of Islamic jurisprudence. He also taught two future founders of the Sunni schools of thought: Abu Hanifa (Hanafi school) and Malik ibn Anas (Maliki school).

Like his ancestors, Imam Jafar was persecuted by both the Umayyads and later the Abbasid Caliphs, which explains his withdrawal from political involvement. Instead, he focused on contributing to the theological foundations of Islam.

Since the establishment of *Imamah* as an institution in 632 CE, Imam Jafar became the first to elaborate on the concept, and to define the key principles of Shia doctrine.

In 765 CE, Imam Jafar was poisoned to death, following the fate of his predecessors. However, unlike them, his death witnessed a pivotal historical moment.

It divided Shia Islam!!

At Imam Jafar's funeral, one notable figure was conspicuously absent: his eldest son and designated successor, Ismail.

It was widely believed that Ismail had died during a revolt against the Abbasids. No public appearances were made by him after Imam Jafar's passing, leading most Shia Muslims to accept his younger brother, Musa al-Kadhim, as the seventh Shia Imam. This group of followers came to be known as the *Ithna'Ashariyya*, or Twelvers as they believe in twelve divinely appointed and infallible Imams.

Meanwhile, a minority of Shia Muslims refused to pledge allegiance to Imam Musa al-Kadhim, believing that the rightful Imam Ismail had not died. Instead owing to persecution, he was hiding in Basra, Iraq.

Ismail being the seventh from Mawla Ali's lineage, his followers came to be known as Seveners apart from being referred to as Ismailis.

Ismailism was born!!

Imam Jafar's death, therefore, marked the permanent division of Shia Islam into two factions: the Twelvers and the Seveners or Ithna'Ashariyya and Ismailis respectively.

From an Islamic perspective, Shia Muslims were already a minority, and after the schism over the seventh Imam, the Ismailis became a minority within that minority. As a result, they faced persecution not only from the Sunni Caliphs but also from the majority Twelver Shia community.

At this point, it is essential to consider the concept of an unbroken chain of Imams, as propounded by the Aga Khan in modern times.

As discussed earlier, on December 13, 1986, the Aga Khan IV ordained a constitution, claiming direct descent from both the Prophet Muhammad and Mawla Ali, thus positioning himself as the rightful Shia Ismaili Imam.

However, for this claim to hold, all forty-seven Imams in this allegedly unbroken chain between him and Mawla Ali must be found in historical records.

Unfortunately for Aga Khan, recorded history does not cooperate!!

The "unbroken chain" first broke with the absence of Ismail, the seventh Imam, and then with the absence of his alleged descendants Mohammad ibn Ismail, Wafi Ahmed, Taqi Mohammad, and Razi din Abdallah.

These Imams either remained hidden or never existed. However, they feature in Aga khan's fictional lineage propounded behind closed doors of the Jamatkhana!

This obscure period from Imam Ismail to Razi din Abdallah is known as *Dawr-i Satr* (the period of concealment).

Dr. Farhad Daftary, an Islamic scholar, writes in his book *The Isma'ilis: Their History and Doctrines:*

"Early Ismailism, or the pre-Fatimid period in Ismaili history, is one of the most obscure major phases in the entire history of Ismailism. The genealogy of the Fatimid caliphs has been a source of numerous controversies, many of which defy satisfactory resolution. According to later

Ismaili doctrine, the ancestors of the Fatimids were the Ismaili Imams who descended from Muhammad ibn Ismail. However, Ismaili sources are highly reluctant to mention the names of these 'hidden Imams,' and the links between Abd Allah al-Mahdi and Muhammad ibn Ismail remain shrouded in mystery. The names of these figures are not found in the earliest Ismaili sources that have come to light."

Fatimid Caliphate

*D*awr i Satr lasted 144 years!!

Then the period of concealment came to an end when an Ismaili figure, Abd Allah al-Mahdi, declared himself a descendant of elusive Ismail.

During the *Dawr-i Satr*, Ismailis, lived and died underground. However, as a movement, not only did they survive but discreetly propagated their faith.

Imam Jafar's foresight had equipped them with the means to protect themselves from widespread persecution. He introduced the concept of *taqiyya,* (hiding of religious identity) This would safeguard their lives and property in hostile circumstances.

For Ismailis, *taqiyya* became a crucial survival mechanism during the Middle Ages as it remains to the day. It is worth noting that over the centuries, the application of *taqiyya* within Ismailism has evolved significantly, as will be discussed in later chapters.

Under the cover of *taqiyya* during the *Dawr-i Satr,* Ismailis laid the foundation for a Shia Caliphate, marking a golden period in Ismaili history.

This began with the efforts of Abu Abdallah al-Shi'i, an Ismaili missionary in North Africa. Al-Shi'i successfully converted the local Kutama Berber tribe to the Ismaili cause and led them to conquer Ifriqiya (a historical region of North Africa, encompassing parts of modern-day Tunisia, Tripolitania, and Algeria).

Around the same period, Abdallah al-Mahdi, a Syrian Ismaili declared himself the hidden Ismaili Imam. Due to the Abbasid persecution in Syria, al-Mahdi fled to Sijilmasa, Morocco, adopting *taqiyya.*

However, the Sunni ruler of Morocco, tipped off by the Abbasids, soon discovered his identity and had him arrested. When Al-Shi'i learnt of Imam's arrest, he set out for Sijilmasa and liberated him.

In 910 CE, Imam al-Mahdi arrived in Raqadda, Tunisia where he received a royal welcome. Here, he declared himself the Caliph. Soon every mosque in his Caliphate began delivering a *khutba* (formal sermon) in his name, Al-Mahdi Billah (the Imam rightly guided by God) and Amir al-mu'minin (Commander of the Faithful)

For the first time since Mawla Ali, a Shia Imam had ascended the throne of Caliphate!

The new Caliphate was named the Fatimid Caliphate, after Fatima, the daughter of the Prophet Muhammad, to whom al-Mahdi claimed descent.

The *Dawr-i Satr* had come to an end, and to the relief of Ismailis, *Dawr-i Kashf* (period of revelation) had begun.

Over 186 years, eight Ismaili Imams ruled the Fatimid Caliphate. At its height, the Caliphate extended from the western reaches of Asia to North Africa, stretching from the Mediterranean to the Red Sea in the east.

The Impostor

Although the Ismailis were now free to breath fresh air, the identity of their Imam and Caliph, al-Mahdi, remained shrouded in mystery.

To clarify his lineage, al-Mahdi sent a letter to his disciples in Yemen, establishing his identity as an Ismaili Imam and attempting to explain the mystery of the "hidden Imams" during the *Dawr-i Satr.*

However, the letter raised more questions than answers!!

Instead of tracing his lineage through Ismail, al-Mahdi claimed descent from Abdallah, the half-brother of Ismail. Additionally, al-Mahdi's penchant for wine and luxury contrasted sharply with the expectations of a divine figure.

The suspicion deepened!

Abu Abdallah al-Shi'i, the architect of Fatimid Caliphate, and other Ismaili leaders were deeply disappointed to discover that the individual for whom they had shed blood was, in fact, not the awaited Imam al-Mahdi.

As a result in 912 CE, a revolt broke out, and many prominent missionaries, army officers, and leaders defected. In response, Imam al-Mahdi placed his son, al-Qaim, in charge of the army, who successfully suppressed the uprising.

Tragically, Abu Abdallah al-Shi'i fell to the very sword he had entrusted to the imposter, al-Mahdi.

Eventually, Ismaili Imam and Caliph, al-Mahdi passed away in 934 CE at the age of sixty-one.

Decline of Fatimid Empire

Since the establishment of Fatimid Caliphate back in 910 CE in Tunisia, the capital had moved to Egypt. Here they had founded a city that we know today as Cairo.

It was here that the last Ismaili Caliph, Al-Mustansir bi'llah was born on July 16, 1029. He had inherited the Caliphate and Ismaili Imamate as a seven-year-old child.

Rasad, a Nubian slave, governed state affairs until the child Caliph came of age. Although Al-Mustansir's reign extended for fifty-eight years, he became the last Ismaili Imam, to rule over Fatimid Caliphate.

Under Al-Mustansir, the Fatimids lost significant territory. Internal strife within the army undermined their defenses. As a result, the Seljuks of Persia had seized most of the Levant, the Normans had taken Sicily, and Arab forces made headway in North Africa.

Besides, Al-Mustansir's court was dominated by corrupt military officials who depleted the treasury. Nature also contributed to the Caliph's woes given the empire was gripped by famine and plague during his times.

The Caliphate was engulfed by anarchy!

To restore order, Al-Mustansir turned to Badar al-Jamali, a Palestinian governor, for assistance. Jamali quelled the unrest and revitalized the economy. In recognition of his efforts, Al-Mustansir conferred upon him the title of *vizier* (high-ranking minister). However, with time Jamali amassed enough power to become the de facto ruler of Egypt, overshadowing the Caliph.

When Jamali died in 1094, his son, al-Afdal, succeeded him and continued to exercise significant control over the government.

Al-Afdal's influence was so extensive that he determined the next Caliph's succession.

In 1094 CE, Al-Mustansir passed away at the age of sixty-five.

His death marked the official end of Ismaili rule over the Fatimid Caliphate and set in motion a division within the Ismaili community.

Legacy of the Fatimid Caliphate

The Ismaili Caliphs, with the notable exception of the Al-Hakim, known as "Mad Caliph," were largely tolerant and inclusive toward people of other faiths. Their meritocratic policies allowed Christians and Jews to occupy prominent positions within the government, fostering a climate of relative religious harmony.

Among their most enduring legacies were the founding of Cairo, one of the great cities of the medieval world, and the establishment of Al-Azhar University, which remains a symbol of the importance they placed on education and intellectual advancement.

The Ismailis also left behind a rich architectural and artistic heritage that continues to endure in Egypt and Tunisia. Notable examples include Al-Hakim Mosque, and the Mosque of Al-Salih Tala'i as testaments to the cultural and religious vibrancy of the Fatimid era.

The Fatimids also contributed to Islamic intellectual tradition, particularly in the fields of theology and Shi'i thought. Works by scholars such as Abu Yaqub al-Sijistani and Hamid al-Kirmani, especially in metaphysics, are noteworthy contributions to Islamic philosophy.

Indeed, Fatimid Caliphate was a golden period for the Ismailis, one that produced influential thinkers whose impact extended beyond their time and shaped the future of both Islam and Ismailism.

One such notable figure was Nasir Khusraw, a philosopher, poet, and traveler who remains a towering figure in Persian literature.

Nasir Khusraw

Nasir Khusraw was born in 1004 CE in Qubadiyan, a district of Balkh (present-day Afghanistan). Widely regarded as one of the greatest Persian poets, he was also a philosopher whose works continue to be celebrated in literary and intellectual circles today.

His most famous works include *Safar-nama* (a travelogue), *Zad al-Musafirin* and *Kitab Jami al-Hikmatayn* (philosophical treatises), as well as *Diwan* (a collection of poems) These literary gems offer invaluable insights into his life and the cultural landscape of his time.

At the age of around forty, Nasir embarked on a pilgrimage to Mecca, which marked the beginning of an extensive journey that spanned the next seven years.

During this period, he traveled across Persia, Syria, and Palestine. Upon reaching Cairo, Nasir was appointed as an Ismaili *da'i* (missionary) by Caliph-Imam al-Mustansir.

In 1052 CE, Nasir began his *da'wa* (religious propagation) activities in Persia, particularly in Khurasan and Nishapur, operating under the noses of Ismaili adversaries such as the Seljuk Sultans, the Sunni rulers of Persia.

After his return to Balkh, Nasir was declared a heretic, forcing him to seek refuge in the valley of Yumgan, a mountainous district in eastern Afghanistan. There, he spent the remainder of his life propagating Ismailism until his death around 1089 CE.

His tomb, situated on a hillock in present-day Hadrat-i-Said, remains a site of reverence. Central Asian Ismailis continue to revere him for introducing Ismailism to the region and leaving behind a legacy of *qasidas,* devotional hymns that are still cherished.

Chapter 3

The Nizari Ismailism

In 1095 CE, after the death of Al-Mustansir, the eighth Fatimid Ismaili Caliph, a bitter succession struggle ensued. Nizar, the eldest son of Caliph was poised to ascend as the next Caliph and Ismaili Imam.

However, *vizier* al-Afdal, who had amassed considerable power, bypassed Nizar in favor of his younger brother Al-Musta'li.

The *vizier* after all was Al Mustali's father-in-law!!

Nizar revolted but he was swiftly overpowered and condemned to a slow, painful death in prison.

This led to a crisis like the Shi'i schism of the eighth century when the Shi'a community had split between the *Ithna'Ashariyya* and Ismaili branches.

This time, the Ismailis themselves split between the supporters of Nizar and Al-Musta'li. The followers of Nizar would later become known as Nizari Ismailis, led by the Aga Khan in modern times, while the Musta'li faction eventually became known as the Bohra community.

At this juncture, it is appropriate to review Aga khan IV's Ismaili Constitution. In this public document he had claimed to be the forty ninth Imam of Ismaili Muslims.

But are his followers the only Ismailis in the world?

After the split of Shia Muslims between *Ithna'Ashariyya* and Ismaili branches, Ismailism fragmented into several sub sects such as Druze, Qarmatians, Nizaris, Must-e-alians. Of these and others, only Nizaris recognize Agakhan as their spiritual leader.

For Aga khan to claim to be an Ismaili Imam is not only preposterous but an affront to the belief systems of other Ismailis around world!!

At any rate, much like the earlier disappearance of Imams during *Dawr e Satr*, Imam Nizar's son, Al-Hadi, also vanished without a trace. Interestingly, he features on the Aga Khan's list of "unbroken chain of Imams."

According to Dr. Farhad Daftary in *Ismailis: Their History and Doctrines,* Nizar himself did not designate a successor, which led to confusion among his followers. Daftary notes:

"However, Nizar himself does not seem to have designated any of his sons as his successor. As a result, about a year after al-Mustansir's death, the Nizari's were left without an accessible imam as their leader."

The disappearance of Al Hadi marked the beginning of the second era of *Dawr-i Satr,* or the period of concealment. During this period of uncertainty and insecurity, the Nizari Ismailis were more focused on surviving the Musta'lian sword than on locating their missing Imam Al Hadi.

They were desperately in search of a haven and…they found it!!

The Rise of Hassan ibn Sabbah

Born in 1034 CE in an *Ithna'Ashariyya* family in Qom, Iran, Hassan converted to Ismailism at the age of seventeen, influenced by the teachings of *da'i* Abdul Malik Attash. Soon after, he became deeply involved in Ismaili propagation.

Hassan Ibn Sabbah was one of the greatest political strategists of his time. In addition to his expertise in politics, he was also proficient in mathematics, theology, philosophy, and astronomy.

In 1078, Hassan traveled to Cairo, where his knowledge and devotion earned him the rank of *da'i* at the court of the Fatimid Caliph al-Mustansir. Upon returning to Persia in 1081, Hassan embarked on an extensive *da'wa* (propagation of faith) mission.

His travels took him to the Daylam district in Persia, where he encountered the fortress of Alamut, perched high on a jagged outcrop in the Alburz mountains. This stronghold, seemingly impregnable, would become immortalized in Nizari Ismaili culture and literature.

At the time, Alamut was held by an *Alid* named Zaydi Mahdi, who was serving as a representative of the Seljuk Sultan, Malikshah. Unbeknownst to Mahdi, his soldiers defected to Hassan's cause.

In 1090, Hassan, disguised as a teacher, infiltrated the fortress, rallied the local inhabitants, and successfully ousted Mahdi. With Alamut now under his control, Hassan set about seizing additional fortresses, including Mansurakuh, Mihrnigar, Ustunawand, and the strategically significant Girdkuh.

These victories proved critical to the survival of the Ismaili movement.

As discussed, a succession crisis unfolded in Cairo in 1095 after the demise of Al-Mustansir billah, the Ismaili Imam and Caliph. His son Nizar had been immured to death while his family and supporters found themselves vulnerable to the threat of annihilation.

It was in these volatile times that Hassan's stronghold in Alamut provided refuge for the Egyptian Nizari Ismailis. Those who remained behind in Cairo had no choice but to practice *taqiyya* (concealment of their beliefs) to avoid detection.

Nizari Settlement in Persia

While the Nizari Ismailis had found shelter in Alamut, Persia, they continued to live in constant fear of retribution from Sultan Malik Shah. After all, they were illegally occupying his territory.

Their fears proved justified when the Sultan soon launched an invasion to reclaim the fortress. However, he failed to evict Nizaris owing to Alamut's high strategic position and near-impenetrable defenses.

Although his illegal settlement had survived the Seljuk invasion, Hassan was wise enough to acknowledge that it was only a matter of time before the Sultan would find a way to dislodge them.

But what could Hassan do to protect the Nizari settlement? Was a military confrontation feasible given he had a fraction of Sultan's mighty military force?

Soon, Hassan devised a strategy. It was non-confrontational but rooted in terror and psychological warfare.

But where did he find inspiration for such a strategy? Likely, he looked to the zealots of the Roman era, particularly the Sicarii, a splinter group of the Jewish political movement. The Sicarii were known for their acts of public assassination, targeting Roman officials and instilling widespread fear introducing the concept of political terrorism to the ancient world.

Paradise

Hassan sought to not only revive but immortalize terrorism as a tool of resistance.

His plan was simple yet effective: young men, disguised as *dervishes* (Sufi saints), would infiltrate public

spaces and assassinate high-ranking political, military, religious, and government officials.

Hassan hoped that the shock and terror of these public killings would destabilize the Persian establishment and drive them to leave the Nizaris in peace.

However, the success of this plan relied heavily on the willingness of the recruits to carry out such dangerous missions.

How could Hassan convince his young followers to walk into a market, kill someone, and expect to survive? How could he persuade them to die for Nizari cause? Would his men go on suicide missions?

Soon his ingenuity found a solution!!

Hassan would disguise proposed acts of terrorism as martyrdom with a promise of heaven. Legend has it that Hassan constructed a physical representation of paradise in his hideout at Alamut.

The recruits were lured with flowing rivers of milk, fruit-laden orchards, and seventy-two female virgins awaiting them. These Quranic descriptions were augmented with *hashish* (cannabis), which induced a state of euphoria in the young men. In this altered state, Hassan convinced them that martyrdom would open the gates to the real paradise in the afterlife.

This blend of religious imagery, euphoric experience, and the allure of paradise provided the psychological motivation Hassan needed to turn his followers into zealots, willing to die for Nizari cause.

Order of Assassins

Hassan would refer to his mentally captivated recruits as *Fidayeens* (plural for Fidai: someone willing to die for something or someone) However to the world outside of their hideout in Alamut, the brainwashed recruits became known as the infamous *Hashisheens* (users of cannabis) The term over time evolved into the Assassins, the familiar word for a killer.

Assassin loyalty and dedication to Nizari cause was unquestionable. Legend has it that they would leap to their deaths from a cliff upon Hassan's command.

Trained in a range of combat techniques, disguises, and both psychological and physical strategies, the assassins were ready to carry out suicide attacks on those who threatened their settlement.

The streets of Isfahan soon ran red with blood!! Numerous officials of the Seljuk empire were assassinated in broad daylight.

Then the highlight of the entire operation eventuated!!

In 1092, Nizar al-Mulk, the Sultan's Prime Minister, was stabbed to death by assassins!

Although the entire Seljuk empire was now gripped by terror, the assassins did not relent. They extended the spread of panic across neighboring regions, culminating in the assassination of Conrad, King of Jerusalem, who was stabbed to death by assassins disguised as monks.

Hassan's designs had proved to be effective. He had successfully sent a message to his adversaries that though the Nizaris were few, their ability for shock tactics, capacity for violence and suicidal determination made them a force to be reckoned with.

From that point onward, the Nizari came to be known by a chilling moniker, the "Order of Assassins."

Marco Polo's Account

The famous Venetian explorer Marco Polo, who traveled through the region encountered the Legend of Assassins. He provides a vivid account of this in his renowned work *The Travels of Marco Polo*. The book offers a fascinating glimpse into the mind of Hassan ibn Sabbah:

"In a beautiful valley between two lofty mountains, he [Hassan] formed a luxurious garden, stocked with every kind of delicious fruit and fragrant shrub that could be procured. Palaces of various sizes and designs were erected within the garden... The inhabitants of these palaces were elegant and beautiful damsels, skilled in singing, playing musical instruments, dancing, and particularly in the arts of dalliance and amorous allure... At his court, likewise, this chief entertained several youths. He frequently discoursed with them about the paradise promised by the Prophet. At certain times, he caused cannabis to be administered to ten or a dozen of these youths. When half-dead with sleep, they were carried to the various apartments of the palaces in the garden. Upon awakening, each one found himself surrounded by lovely damsels, singing, playing, and offering the most seductive caresses. They were served with delicate foods and exquisite wines. Intoxicated by this indulgence,

they believed they had entered Paradise. After spending four or five days in this euphoria, they were once again rendered unconscious and carried out of the garden. When questioned by Hassan about their experience, their answer was always, 'In Paradise, through the favor of Your Highness.' To these youths, Hassan would then say: 'We have the assurances of our Prophet that he who defends his lord shall inherit Paradise. If you show yourselves devoted to my service, that glorious fate awaits you.'"

(The Travels of Marco Polo, Book 1, Chapter XXII)

Yaum-e Qiyama

Though Hassan had successfully secured the Nizari stronghold at Alamut, a troubling question lingered: what good was it to have a physical sanctuary without the guidance of a divinely appointed Imam?

According to Shia doctrine, the Imam must always be present, both spiritually and physically, to guide the faithful.

But where was the Imam?

The physical absence of Al-Hadi, the son of the slain Imam Nizar, cast doubt on the very foundations of Nizari belief system.

Was he dead like his father, or had he gone hiding?

Anthony Campbell, in his influential work *The Assassins of Alamut*, writes:

"Until the end of his long life, Hassan remained in Alamut, a solitary and austere figure, overseeing his strange realm, ordering assassinations, writing, planning, and waiting. But waiting for what? Did he believe that the son of the deceased Nizar, al-Hadi, would one day reappear to claim the Imamat? If so, how would he be recognized as the true Imam?"

Eventually, in 1124, Hassan died in his Alamut hideout...without meeting the Imam of the time, Al Hadi!!

His death marked the end of a turbulent chapter for the Nizari Ismaili community. His lieutenant, Kiya Buzurg Ummeed, took over the leadership of Alamut, followed by his descendants, who continued to watch the horizon from the fort's window, waiting for the elusive Imam al-Hadi to appear.

For sixty-seven years, no sign of the Imam ever came, and Nizaris were beginning to wonder!!

Finally, in a desperate move, Hassan II, a descendant of Ummeed, seized control of the Nizari state. First, he declared himself the *hujja,* or authorized representative, of the missing Imam. He claimed to be in communication with Al-Hadi, receiving guidance from an undisclosed location.

Then, Hassan II did what the self-proclaimed Imam Al-Mahdi had done in the 10th century.

He declared himself the Imam of the Nizari Ismailis!!

On 8 August 1164, during the month of Ramadan, Hassan II invited dignitaries from across the Nizari territories to Alamut. There, he announced that he was the Imam, the divinely appointed leader and that he had come to liberate the Nizaris from the rule of *Sharia* (Islamic) law. Then he invited the fasting believers to break their fast at midday, which was a sacrilegious act according to Islamic tenets.

To bolster his claim, he denied that Muhammad ibn Kiya Buzurg Ummeed, his father, was truly his biological parent. Instead, he proclaimed that he was the son of a secret descendant of Imam Nizar, who had allegedly lived hidden in Persia.

This assertion was highly dubious!!

Until that point, Hassan II had publicly acknowledged Muhammad ibn Kiya Buzurg Ummeed as his father. Furthermore, there was no logical reason for his purported father to have lived in secrecy given a fortified stronghold like Alamut.

This event, which became known as *Yaum-e Qiyama* or 'the Day of Resurrection', symbolized the supposed revival of Nizari Ismailism, albeit in a form manipulated for political gain.

Having a living Imam, real or not, was a comforting notion for the Nizari community, who had long awaited such a figure.

However, this brief period of revival and celebration would soon come to a tragic end.

The Mongol Invasion

The Mongol Empire founded by Genghis Khan in 1206 evolved to become the largest contiguous empire in world history. Owing to their unparalleled ferocity, strategy and the use of terror, they ruled territories from the Sea of Japan to Eastern Europe and from the Arctic to the Indian subcontinent.

As David Nicole notes in *The Mongol Warlords,*

"Terror and mass extermination of anyone opposing them was a well-tested Mongol tactic."

When faced with resistance, Mongol leaders would employ total war, resulting in the widespread slaughter of civilian populations and the obliteration of cities and resources.

Over 162 years, an estimated 40 million people were killed during Mongol campaigns, from Genghis Khan's rise in 1206 to Toghon Temur's reign in 1368.

In 1246, when the Mongols turned their sights on Persia, the twenty-sixth Nizari Imam, Ala ad-Din Muhammad, found himself and his people in immediate peril.

With the Mongols closing in, the Imam feared for the survival of Alamut. Desperate to avoid annihilation, he sought to form alliance with neighboring Christian territories, arguing that the Mongols were a common enemy. However, the proposal was swiftly rejected, as the Christians, saw Muslims as their adversaries including the Nizari Ismailis.

Faced with rejection from the Christians, the Imam had no choice but to attempt to appease the Mongols. In

1246, after Guyuk Khan ascended to the Mongol throne, Imam Ala ad-Din sent ambassadors to Mongolia, offering a hand of friendship. Sadly, the great Khan dismissed the ambassadors and ordered Hulegu Khan to fast track of Alamut's invasion.

Imam's diplomacy had backfired!!

Furthermore, his failed diplomacy created a rift between him and his commanders. Soon, Imam's dead body was found in suspicious circumstances.

The Fall of Alamut

Upon his father's death in 1230, twenty-five-year-old Ruknuddin Khurshah ascended as the new Nizari Imam.

In the past, Ismailis and Nizaris had experienced persecution and killings, but the new Imam was facing extermination of the entire Nizari settlement in Persia!!

These were unprecedented times.

Never had Ismailis been exposed to threats to life such as the imminent Mongol invasion. True to his reputation, Hulegu Khan spared no effort in pillaging and slaughtering the Nizari Ismailis.

Realizing that surrender was the only option left, the young Imam chose to delay the inevitable. Instead of confronting Hulegu directly, he took refuge in the Maymun-diz fortress and sent his brother, Shahanshah, with a message of symbolic submission to the Khan.

Hulegu, unmoved by the gesture, demanded that the Imam destroy his castles before surrendering in person. The Imam, unwilling to comply, attempted a different tactic. He sent his young son to the Mongol leader, hoping to appeal to Hulegu's emotions. However, the Khan returned the boy unharmed, reinforcing his demand for the Imam's submission.

Desperate to survive in the face of death, this time Imam Khurshah sent his younger brother, Shiranshah, with 300 men, hoping once more to sway Hulegu. But the Khan remained resolute.

On 18 November 1256, Hulegu began his siege of Maymun-diz, launching a large-scale bombardment and intensifying his demand for surrender.

Ultimately, Imam Khurshah relented and descended from his castle, walking toward what he believed would be his death.

But to his surprise, Hulegu received him with unexpected courtesy.

The Khan's primary goal was the destruction of the Imam's fortresses and castles, after which he would dispose of the Nizari leader.

At Hulegu's command, Imam Khurshah issued a *Farman*—an edict—ordering the demolition of all forty Nizari castles. Once the task was completed, the Imam's fate was sealed.

On 9 March 1256, Imam and his followers were sent to Mongolia to the court of Mongke Khan, where they were executed.

Meanwhile, back in Persia and Syria, Hulegu's forces massacred nearly 100,000 Nizari Ismailis in a brutal campaign of annihilation.

The sun had set on the Nizari state, which had been founded 166 years earlier by the genius of Hasan ibn Sabbah.

Once again, just like their ancestors in Arabia and North Africa, the Nizari Ismailis found themselves vulnerable, under a heavy cloud of persecution.

Once again, they retreated into the shadows of obscurity.

Book 2

Divorcing Islam

Chapter One

Mission India

The period between the eleventh and thirteenth centuries was turbulent for the Nizari Ismailis. They had witnessed the division of Ismailism into Nizari and Must-e- alian factions, followed by the immurement of Imam Nizar. Then to escape the Must-e-alian sword they once again found themselves underground practicing *taqiyya*. This marked the beginning of second *Dawr e Satr* and finally the Mongols obliterated the entire Nizari state in Persia.

Yet, despite it all, Nizaris proved to be resilient.

Much like Hasan ibn Sabbah, who had established a Nizari state in Alamut, another Nizari *da'i*, Syed Nooruddin Mohammad, arrived in India seeking a new foothold and much needed source of revenue.

But why India?

Why would Hindus subscribe to an Islamic ideology? Wouldn't finding refuge in a Muslim territory have been more pragmatic for the Nizaris, given the stark contrasts between Hindu religious beliefs, cultural outlooks, and linguistic traditions with Islam?

Convincing the Hindus was undeniably a daunting task, yet it proved to be a more viable option. Propagating within a Muslim territory was fraught with the risk of persecution due to their heretical beliefs assigning divinity to their Imam.

In contrast, the Hindus were open to the concept of a human God. After all, they have worshipped the human incarnation of the divine from times immemorial. Furthermore, they were profoundly religious and generously funded their deities.

More importantly, India was the richest economy in the medieval world. It was no wonder that it had been the target of Persian bandits like Yaqub ibn Saffrid and Mahmud of Ghazni long before the Ismaili schism of the eleventh century.

Although the Nizaris had done their homework, they were not bandits like Saffrid or Ghazni. If anything, they were a more cautious group, fearful people practicing *taqiyya* due to their history of enduring persecution. Therefore, their modus operandi was to operate clandestinely and deceive just as they had done in the past and continue to do today.

At any rate, the Indian mission looked promising, but it had to be executed with extreme secrecy. After all, this time they were about to make an unprecedented move!!

Their Imam was about to assume the identity of Vishnu, a Hindu God!

To Muslims this would mean heresy of the highest order, a just reason to persecute Nizaris.

Das avatar (Ten Incarnations)

According to Hindu scriptures, Vishnu, the Preserver, is depicted as a divine entity resting beneath the hood of the serpent Shesha, floating in the ocean of milk, known as Kshira Sagara, accompanied by his consort, Lakshmi.

It is believed that whenever evil disrupts the cosmic order, Vishnu descends to Earth in various *avataras* (incarnations) to restore balance. Since time immemorial, it is believed he has incarnated in nine distinct *avataras:*

1. Matsya – the fish
2. Kurma – the turtle
3. Varaha – the wild boar
4. Narasimha – a creature that is part man, part lion
5. Vamana – the dwarf

6. Parashurama – the warrior
7. Rama – the upright ruler, revered as Lord Rama
8. Krishna – the sagacious strategist, revered as Lord Krishna
9. Buddha – the enlightened being

Hindus are still awaiting the arrival of Kalki, the tenth and final avatar, who would introduce a new order of existence. According to Vedic astronomical calculations, Kalki is expected to appear in 4,30,000 years, riding a horse with a flaming sword.

These ten incarnations, or *das avatara*, have captivated the minds of Hindus since times immemorial!

Given this backdrop, it is not hard to infer that the displaced Nizaris saw an opportunity.

Why not hasten the arrival of Kalki and present the Nizari Imam as the tenth avatar?

The idea was a double-edged sword!

Although, there was distinct possibility of financial rewards and a haven but if detected, it could provoke Hindu backlash. Their stakes were higher if the Muslims were to discover them associating their Imam with Vishnu.

That would be catastrophic!!

To assert that a Muslim Imam was a Hindu God would be an extreme example of *Shirk*, the only sin considered unforgivable according to the Holy Quran.

But then what choice did the Nizaris have?

It was a do-or-die situation!

Pir Satgur Noor

In the early twelfth century, with a sword hanging over his neck, *Da'i* Syed Nooruddin Mohammad arrived in Patan, in the western Indian state of Gujarat. Here, he would become known as Pir Satgur Noor, "the enlightened and true master."

The linchpin of Pir's propagation strategy were the *ginans* (devotional hymns, meaning gnosis), which the Pir allegedly composed to herald the good news of Kalki's arrival sooner than expected.

Though his Kalki *ginans* did not survive the test of time, the works of future Pirs on the topic did. In addition to the core message of Kalki's arrival, the *ginans* were also used as a tool to invoke devotion and promote the Nizari doctrine.

In modern times, Aga Khan devotees believe that the *ginans* were the result of their Pir's accumulated knowledge of Indian culture, languages, dialects, *shastriya sangeet* (classical music), and numerous ideologies and theologies.

However, according to scholarly research, this is more a belief than a historical reality. Dr. Farhad Daftary, in his book *Isma'ilis: Their History and Doctrines*, writes:

"Much controversy surrounds the authorship of the ginans, which is generally ascribed to a few early missionaries, or pirs as dais were called in the Indian subcontinent."

Professor W. Ivanow, a well-known Russian scholar and respected researcher of Ismaili history, similarly writes in his book *Ismaili Literature a Bibliographical Survey:*

"The great majority of ginans are the creation of anonymous authors. Apparently, quite a considerable proportion of those attributed to the authorship of the Great Pirs probably have nothing to do with them and were composed at a much later date. This particularly applies to the ginans about various Pirs, their miracles, and their sayings."

Despite this, the followers of Aga Khan maintain a different perspective. Not only do they believe that the *ginans* are miraculous works authored by their Pirs, but they also consider the content to be an interpretation of the Holy Quran.

Aga Khan III once stated that "*ginans* represent the *tafsir* (interpretation) of the Quran-e-Shariff," Aga Khan IV on his part, endorsed them as a "wonderful tradition." It is no wonder that *ginans* are an intrinsic part of their culture, holding a special place in the religious practice in modern times.

Though they are recited in the *Jamatkhanas* with great affection and fervor, the contents of these *ginans* have the potential to reignite Muslim persecution if their highly controversial, *shirk-infested* themes concealed behind the Indian languages of medieval times were ever to be fully discovered by the wider Muslim ummah. In today's age of rapid information exchange, this possibility has become even more real.

Dancing Statues

Pir Satgur Noor, according to legend, was not only a proficient composer of *ginans* but a singer, a dancer and miracle maker!!

Legend has it that one day, the Pir entered a Hindu temple. Naturally, the Hindu priest did not appreciate his presence, as the Pir appeared to be a Muslim saint. When he was prevented from entering, the Pir clarified that he merely wished to seek advice from the statue gods. The Hindu priest dismissed the Pir as a madman.

How could statues speak to anyone, he thought.

But to his astonishment, the statues began speaking at the Pir's command. Soon, they were dancing to his tunes, and the surrounding stones began to play music.

The news spread like wildfire!

The story culminates with the Hindu king, Siddhraja Jaisingh, arriving to witness the miracle and, ultimately, joining the Nizari Ismaili faith along with his entire kingdom.

The Pir documented this miracle in his ginan, *Satgur Noor na Putla* ("The Statues of Satgur Noor")

It is believed that Pir Satgur Noor proselytized many Hindus from the Lohanas, Kharwa, Kanbi, and Kori castes, bestowing upon them a new name, *Khawaja,* meaning "saint." Over time, however, this venerable title was corrupted to Khoja, the term used today to refer to Aga Khan devotees originating from India.

Eventually, the Pir passed away in Navsari, Gujarat, on an unknown date, but not before laying the foundation for a lasting Nizari Ismaili presence in India, which endures to this day.

Besides, Pir Satgur Noor's legacy inspired many generations of Pirs in the subcontinent, who continued to propagate the Nizari faith for a few centuries into the future.

Pir Shams

Born in Sabzwar, Persia, Pir Shams is also known as Pir Shams Sabzwari. His works suggest that he lived during the Imamate of Nizari Imam Kassim Shah.

His mission took him to many regions such as China, Tibet, Badakhshan, Nepal, Kashmir, Sindh, Gujarat, and

Punjab where he converted numerous individuals to the Nizari faith.

Pir Shams immensely contributed to the Nizari cause by not only composing innumerable *ginans* but also *garbis,* folk songs of Gujarat, through which he spread the Nizari message. It is believed that he sang twenty-eight *garbi* songs over ten consecutive nights during Dusshera, a Hindu festival celebrating Lord Rama's victory over the demon Ravana.

However, his most important work from proselytization perspective is *Pir Shams jo Das Avataar*, a *ginan* depicting early arrival of Kalki.

Jamatkhana

Islam since its inception has fragmented into 73 sects. However, 1400-year-old Islamic tradition holds that any Muslim, regardless of denomination has been welcomed to pray in any mosque across the globe.

(*A notable exception however are Ahmadis who are considered non-Muslims by mainstream Islamic Ummah. This leaves them no choice but to pray in their own mosques*)

Nizaris like any other Muslims prayed in mosques rubbing shoulders with their Muslim brethren. But that changed when Pir Satgur Noor fused Vishnu, the Hindu God with the person of Nizari Ismaili Imam, thus creating a new religious denomination....one of a cultish nature!!

But how did Nizaris in India survive the backlash, given Vishnu's entry in Islamic fold was the ultimate insult, not only to Muslims but also to Hindus?

There was only one way and that was to practice heresy behind closed doors!!

It took the genius of Pir Shams to conceptualize, design and establish a discreet place of worship. He named it *Jamatkhana,* meaning "house of assembly" in Persian.

It could only be accessed by Khojas of India.

The Pir would hide Vishnu, not only behind the protected walls of the *Jamatkhana* but behind the obscurity and inaccessibility of *ginans.*

This strategy proved to be successful as Muslims to date remain blissfully oblivious of Vishnu's presence in the *Jamatkhanas* around the world.

While the *Jamatkhana* provided a discreet physical space for worship, the ever-evolving Nizari faith also required a spiritual framework that would allow adherents to practice their new beliefs. To this end, Pir Shams shaped the direction of Nizari Ismailism, drawing inspiration from mystical aspect of Islam.

Sufism

It is God who has sent down to you the book: In it are verses clear (muhkamat), they are the foundation of the book, others are unspecific (mutashabihat).

Surah Al e Imran: Ayat 7

To communicate with humanity, Muslims believe God sent down Quranic commands that are easily understood. However, a few of these commands are of an esoteric nature and hence difficult to comprehend.

Naturally, Muslims have followed the exoteric meaning of the Quran, except those involved in *tassawwuf* (Sufism), a mystical aspect of Islam.

Sufis believe that God can be understood through a spiritual connection between the seeker and the prophet, and his message. To comprehend the *Sunna* (legacy) of the Prophet, one must connect with a legitimate Shaykh a venerable figure tracing his lineage to the Prophet. Therefore, Sufi allegiance and veneration go to the

Shaykh of their time, forming a *murid-murshid* (disciple-master) relationship.

Sufis gather in a *khanaqah,* a special place of worship, to study the esoteric aspects of the Quran, practice *dhikr* (the repeated chanting of God's name) and importantly, the exoteric aspects of Islam.

Their goal being *fana fillah*…. becoming one with God.

Pir Shams took a deep interest in Sufism. He incorporated elements such as *Dhikr* into the foundation of his newly found cult, aiming to create a Sufi and spiritual appearance. Most importantly, he established a *murid-murshid* relationship to bind the followers to their Imam.

However, exoteric practices, represented by the Five Pillars of Islam were deemed too tedious.

Nizaris redesigned them, not only to suit the cult's practices but to make them less cumbersome!!

In their *Shahada,* the cult placed Mawla Ali and hence their current Imam alongside Allah and the Prophet. *Hajj,* the pilgrimage to Mecca, was substituted by a pilgrimage to the *Jamatkhana. Salat*, the obligatory Islamic prayers, would be replaced by *shirk-infested Dua* (prayers invoking the Imam as a divine entity) while *Sawm* (the fasting during Ramadan) would be deemed voluntary.

Most importantly, *Zakat*, the practice of charity, was replaced by *Dasond* which would serve the core objective of the cult.

The religious revenue would now benefit the Imam, not the needy!!

Islamic principles had been modified and hence it was no wonder *Jamatkhana* doors had to remain closed to the public, as they are to this day!!

Miracles of Pir Shams

The great Pir spent the latter part of his illustrious career in Multan, in present-day Pakistan, where he continued the "miraculous" legacy of Pir Satgur Noor.

Riding a paper boat

One legend recounts an incident where Pir Shams' followers were persecuted in Multan by a prominent Sunni saint, Baha ul-Din Zakariya.

Determined to make his presence known, Pir Shams set out to confront him. One day, the Pir arrived at the banks of the river Ravi, hoping to catch a boat to his destination but none were available.

Using his spiritual powers, he magically transformed a piece of paper into a vessel, boarded it, and sailed to Multan!!

When Zakariya learned of the Pir's arrival, he sent him a bowl of milk filled to the brim, symbolizing that the city was already full of saints and had no room for another. In response, Pir Shams placed a single flower atop the bowl and returned it, conveying that there was still room for a flower and its fragrance.

As the boat sailed past Zakariya's house, the saint sat on his balcony. Intent on driving away this unwelcome guest, Zakariya cast an evil eye upon the paper boat, causing it to come to an abrupt halt.

Pir Shams, sensing the interruption, gazed around and spotted Zakariya. In retaliation, the Pir cast a miraculous glance toward Zakariya, and to his horror, two horns suddenly sprouted from his forehead and became fastened to the windowsill.

Despite his best efforts, Zakariya could not free himself. Stricken with fear and remorse, Zakariya sent his sons to Pir Shams, seeking forgiveness.

Pir Shams later narrated this event in his *ginan*:

Na'v kij'e Ali'ke na'm'ki, an'e te mah'e sacha bhari'e bha'r; pavan jo chal'e prem'ka, to Ali utar'e par're.

"Make a boat in the name of Ali, in which fill the load of the truth. If the wind of love blows, Mawla Ali will take you across."

Tiyan Bawadin ne bhundo kari, singada kidha parkash

"He (Pir Shams) exposed Baha u-ddin's evil cast, cursing him with a pair of horns."

The Dead Prince

Having dealt with Zakariya, Pir Shams' mission in Multan gained momentum and received widespread fame and reverence.

After all, who could dismiss the man who sailed on a paper boat and brought the mighty Zakariya to his knees?

The Pir would soon have another opportunity to display his miraculous powers.

The prince of the kingdom fell gravely ill and eventually passed away. The traumatized king summoned the finest physicians and saints, hoping someone could restore the prince to life, but all their efforts proved in vain. It was then that the king's ministry suggested turning to Pir Shams, the miracle worker. If anyone could bring the prince back to life, surely it would be him.

When Pir Shams arrived by the side of the dead prince, he cast a miraculous glance at the lifeless body and uttered,

"*Kum bi Izanillah*" (Rise by the command of God)

Yet, the dead prince remained motionless. Undeterred, the Pir then commanded,

"*Kum bi Izani*" (Rise by my command)

In an instant, the dead prince sprung to life. The king overjoyed and deeply grateful, lavished rewards upon the Pir.

Pir Shams documented this miracle in his *ginan:*

Tare' muvo jivadiyo gurjie, kidha khel anant apaar;

"The Guru gave life to the dead body; Pir Shams says as such."

Skinning of Pir Shams

For Pir Shams, bringing the prince back to life was not a cause for celebration. By performing this miracle, he had transcended the boundaries of Allah's power, an act of *Shirk,* an unforgivable sin in Islam.

The Pirs' adversaries seized this opportunity. A *fatwa* (opinion) was issued, declaring that Pir Shams should be skinned alive for his transgression!

On the appointed day, thousands gathered in an open field to witness the spectacle… the skinning of a living man!!

As the crowd watched with bated breath, *jallad*, the executioner, approached the Pir with a knife. But before he could lay a hand on him, Pir Shams performed another miracle: he removed his own skin from throughout his body, handed it to the executioner, and walked away!!

The crowd was left in stunned silence, jaws agape!!

Sun cooking Pir's meal

Although the saints were humiliated by the skinny miracle, their resolve to rid themselves of Pir Shams only grew stronger. This time they would ostracize him.

*If no one gave him food, he would starve to death….*so they thought!

A decree was issued, and Pir Shams was banned from all essential transactions for survival. For days, he endured extreme hunger and began begging for food in the streets of Multan but to no avail.

One fateful day, while wandering, he passed by a butcher's shop. In an unexpected turn of fortune, the butcher took pity on him and gave him a piece of meat.

But how was the Pir to cook it?

Pir Shams, ever resourceful, decided to bring the sun itself to the earth…to cook the meat!!

He stepped into the open and commanded the sun to descend. The sun, to everyone's astonishment, obeyed, descending lower and lower until the heat became unbearable. The people, unable to withstand the scorching temperatures, fell at the Pir's feet, begging for his forgiveness. Relenting, Pir Shams ordered the sun to return to its rightful place in the sky.

Pir Shams affirmed this miraculous event in his *ginan,* which continues to be recited today—even by PhD-educated followers of the Aga Khan in the information age!!

Tare'suraj mangavio satgurue, te ditho sarve sansar.

"Everyone watched in awe when Satgur ordered the sun to descend."

Ashaji, Shah Shams kero deen pichhano, chaudas tene' payaji; Suraj manga'vi jot dekhadi, nar sohi avatar.

O people! Know the path of Pir Shams, who spread it in all four directions. He summoned the Sun and displayed the Light. He indeed is the manifest Lord.

Pir Shams passed away in 1356 and was buried in Multan, where his mausoleum still stands on the banks of the Ravi River.

His 'miraculous' contributions to the Nizari cause remain unparalleled to this day.

Pir Sadardin

Born around 1300 in Sabzwar, Persia, Pir Sadardin, also known as Sadr-al-din, arrived in India at the age of thirty-five to join his grandfather, Pir Sham's mission.

Pir Sadardin remains one of the most revered Pirs in the history of Nizari Ismailism and continues to hold a prominent place in the hearts and minds of Aga Khan followers in the modern world.

He began his proselytizing efforts in Sindh and gradually expanded his influence on Gujarat. During his lifetime, Pir Sadardin furthered the legacy of Pir Shams. He built numerous *Jamaatkhanas*, appointed *Mukhis* and their assistants *Kamarias* (spiritual leaders) to collect spiritual revenue on behalf of the Imam.

Most importantly he appointed *Vakils* (custodians of spiritual revenue) who would travel on foot from India to Persia to deliver religious dues to the Imam.

The *ginans* he composed were a fusion of various ideologies, blending Islamic, Sufi, Hindu, and occasionally Christian themes.

However, the crowning achievement of his literary work is *Nano Das Avatara* (The Little Ten Incarnations). In this revered work, Pir Sadardin explicitly identifies Mawla Ali as the tenth *avatar of Vishnu.*

Shri Dash Maanhe Shri Dash Maanhe Nakalanki Roope Lidho Chhe Avtaar.

Shri Shaah Mawlaa Murtazaa Ali Roope Naam Bhannaavea ji

"Mawla Ali has incarnated as the 10th Avatara."

Unlike his predecessors, Pir Sadardin relied on storytelling than on making miracles.

Story of a virtuous king

The tale of King Harishchandra and Queen Taramati is a beloved and ancient story familiar to every Hindu child. However, Pir Sadardin adapted and restructured it within his *ginan, Amar te aayo more Shahji jo* to present an example of an ideal follower of the Nizari Imam.

Once upon a time, there lived a brave and virtuous king named Harishchandra of Ayodhya. Although he was known for his virtuous deeds, truthfulness and care for his people, the Gods decided to test him.

Located in the skies, they partnered with a renowned Hindu sage Vishwamitra.

One day, while on a hunting expedition, the king heard a cry for help, as if a woman were in distress. He instinctively turned his horse in the direction of the scream but, in his haste, unknowingly crossed the path of sage Vishwamitra, interrupting his meditation.

The furious sage was ready to curse, when the ever-humble king fell at his feet and begged for forgiveness. Though initially unwilling, the sage finally agreed to pardon the king albeit on a few conditions.

The king would need to relinquish his throne and the palace, live as a common man with his family in the village, and pay 1,000 gold coins to the sage within a month from his own earnings.

The king, unwavering in his commitment to righteousness, agreed to the conditions. He abdicated his throne, forsook his wealth, and left with his wife, Taramati, and son, Rohidas, to live in a village.

However, earning the 1,000 gold coins proved to be an insurmountable challenge. Despite his best efforts, the king could not find work.

As the deadline approached, the king contemplated suicide, but the queen, ever supportive, dissuaded him. To resolve their plight, the queen decided to sell herself and their son to a merchant. Even so, the gold coins remained out of reach.

In a final act of desperation, the king sold himself to a cemetery owner, working as a *chandala* (one who works on funeral pyres)

One day, while performing his duties, the king saw a woman approaching with the corpse of a child in her arms. As she came closer, he realized it was his queen, carrying their son Rohidas's dead body. She requested wood for the cremation, but the king, bound by his role at the cemetery, insisted on payment. The queen, unable to pay, was turned away.

At that moment, sage Vishwamitra miraculously appeared, revealing that he was subjected to a divine test and the Gods were happy with his righteousness. He congratulated the king for his unwavering virtue. With his divine powers, the sage brought the prince back to life, and the family was reunited.

The king, queen and their son rejoicing, returned to their kingdom.

When Pir Sadardin arrived in India to propagate Nizari Ismailism in a new epoch, the legend of Harishchandra was already deeply ingrained in the Indian consciousness.

Pir's version of events presented King Harishchandra as an atheist while his queen, Taramati, as a devout Nizari Ismaili who practiced her faith in secrecy.

As a matter of routine, in the middle of each night, when the king was asleep, the queen would sneak out of the palace. She would ride Hanslo, the king's favorite horse, to attend early morning *Jamatkhana* service.

One night, the king woke up and noticed the queen leaving at odd hours. Suspicion took hold of him, and the following night, he feigned sleep and followed her. Upon learning about her destination, he returned to the palace.

When the queen returned, she was startled to find the king awake. Anxious and unsure of his reaction, she braced herself for the inevitable confrontation.

However, the king shared a dream with her: *"In my dream, I saw you had gone to your parents' house."*

"I have no parents." The queen replied

The king then burst into a fit of anger, demanding to see the contents of the tray she carried. Knowing that the tray contained *juro* (a religious offering), the queen feared the worst.

In desperation, she began praying and surely a miracle occurred before their eyes.

The contents of the tray were transformed into fruit!!

Witnessing this divine intervention, the king recognized that his queen was following the true spiritual path.

Now it was he who wanted to be a Nizari!!

He pleaded with the queen to have him initiate into her faith. The queen, however, warned him that doing so would require great sacrifices: he would need to give his liver, his favorite horse *Hanslo*, and even their son, *Rohidas*.

The king agreed, sacrificing everything, and in doing so, became a Nizari Ismaili. He died a martyr having converted scores to the true faith and achieving salvation.

(Pir Sadardin version is provided in the appendix)

In addition to being a gifted storyteller, Pir Sadardin is credited with inventing the *Khojki* script to protect and preserve the *ginanic* heritage from adversaries.

He made Ucchh (in present-day Pakistan) his headquarters, where he passed away in 1416. His sons, Pir Hasan Kabiruddin and later Pir Tajdin, continued his mission.

End of a tradition

In 1466, Pir Tajdin visited Persia to deliver religious dues to Imam al-Mustansir Billah II on behalf of the *Khojas*. Along with the dues, the devotees had also sent a decorative piece of cloth as a gift for the Imam.

Upon arriving in Persia, the Pir delivered the religious dues and the gift to the Imam. He accepted the dues but gave the piece of cloth to the Pir as a token of his appreciation.

Upon his return to India, the elated Pir had the cloth sewn into a robe for himself. However, when the *jamaat* saw him wearing their gift for the Imam, they accused the Pir of embezzlement.

As a result, the Pir suffered a heart attack and died!!

When Imam al-Mustansir learned of the circumstances surrounding the Pir's death, he was deeply saddened. He decided that the *Khojas* no longer deserved the presence of a saint among them.

Consequently, he did not appoint a new *Pir*. Instead, he sent a collection of his sermons. These were compiled over time into a text known as *Pandiyat e Javanmardi* (Advice of Manliness), which became the Imam's *hujja* (authority)

In conclusion, the *Pirs* had accomplished their Indian mission, they had transformed an Islamic *tariqah* (spiritual path) into a cult in India, and more importantly, they had convinced the *Khoja* disciples to share their incomes with the Imam.

In return, the *Khoja* disciples awaited the promised Kalki.... The tenth avatar of Vishnu!!

For five centuries, Kalki remained elusive but then in 1846, the celestial being arrived in India. However, his arrival did not bring divine peace and order.... rather it disrupted it!!

Chapter 2

The Aga Khans

The forty-fifth Nizari Imam, Khalilullah Ali, was a nobleman from Kahak, Persia. In 1817, a dispute broke out between a group of Nizaris and local shopkeepers, instigated by an *Ithna'ashariyya mullah* (clergyman) named Hussain Yazdi. As tensions escalated into violence, the Nizaris sought refuge in their Imam's residence, but it was stormed by the opposing forces. What followed was an ambush during which Imam Khalilullah Ali was fatally wounded.

The Imam's widow, Bibi Sarkara, pursued justice by bringing the matter before the Persian king, Fateh Ali Shah Qajar. The Shah responded swiftly, ordering the arrest of Yazdi and his accomplices.

Though the incident was tragic, it marked a pivotal moment in the life of the deceased Imam's eldest son and the next Imam in line, Hassan Ali Shah.

In addition to administering justice, the Shah arranged for his daughter, Sarv-i-Jahan Khanum, to marry the thirteen-year-old Imam Hassan, granting him a princely dowry and land holdings. The Imam was later appointed the governor of Qum, and then, Kerman province.

With these titles and privileges, Imam Hassan Ali Shah was now a royal and assumed the honorific alias, Aga Khan, meaning 'lord' or 'master'.

For the next twenty years, Aga khan rolled in the hay. But then…life took a tumultuous turn!

Aga khan became a rebel, a fugitive, a refugee and eventually a mercenary!!

This part of Aga Khan's journey is recounted by his grandson, forty eighth Imam Sultan Mohammad Aga Khan III, in his memoirs:

"In 1838, Aga Khan I found himself in conflict with the ruling Emperor Mohammed Shah. Mr. Justice Arnold provides the following account of the events: 'Hadji Mirza Ahasi, who served as tutor to Mohammed Shah, was also the Prime Minister of Persia throughout the entire reign of his royal pupil, from 1834 to 1848. A Persian of lowly origin, who had once been in the service of Aga Khan, rose to become the chief favorite and minion of the powerful minister. This individual, through his patron, had the audacity to request, in marriage, one of Aga Khan's daughters, a granddaughter of the late Shah-in-Shah. The

Persian historian claims that this demand was perceived by Aga Khan as a great insult, and despite the Prime Minister's insistence, the request was vehemently rejected. Having thus made a bitter enemy of the most powerful man in Persia, Aga Khan likely felt that his only course of action for survival was to take up arms something not uncommon for the great feudatories of an unstable Persia. Establishing Kerman as his headquarters, he continued to fight, albeit with fluctuating fortunes, from 1838 to 1839 and into 1840. However, in that year, overpowered by superior numbers, he was forced to flee. With great difficulty, he made his escape, accompanied by a small band of horsemen.'"

Aga Khan was dismissed from the governorship of Kerman, but he refused to abdicate. Instead, he revolted with the help of his brothers, Sardar Abu'l-Hasan Khan and Muhammad Baqir Khan. Despite their efforts, Aga khan's military resources were no match for the mighty Qajar army. After being imprisoned for eight months, Aga Khan was eventually pardoned by the Shah.

It was a blunder as Aga Khan harbored the ambition to recapture Kerman.

Agakhan I

In 1840, under the pretext of going on Hajj, Aga Khan made his way to Yazd. There, he had secretly arranged for a Nizari force to rise in rebellion against the regime. However, his efforts were thwarted as he was once again outnumbered.

Unlike his previous rebellion, this time his spirit was broken. With a bruised ego and nowhere else to turn, he had no choice but to flee Persia.

Aga Khan wandered through the arid regions of Central Persia and the mountainous terrain of Baluchistan before reaching Afghanistan... desperate for food and shelter.

His arrival in Afghanistan, however, marked a turning point in his life and laid the foundation of Aga Khan dynasty.

Anglo-Afghan War

By the 1830s, the British Empire had colonized vast portions of the globe, but the jewel in its crown was India. It was no wonder its protection was of paramount importance. In 1837, fearing a Russian invasion of India via the Khyber and Bolan passes, the British made Afghanistan a key geopolitical target. Their plan was to install a local Emir as a puppet ruler to maintain control over the region.

Coincidentally, in 1838, a succession dispute between two Afghan dynasties, the Barakzais and Durranis erupted. The British invaded Afghanistan on the pretext of supporting Barakzai Dost Mohammad. However, they underestimated the resolve of the Durranis, who proved to be a formidable force. Now, the British found themselves desperately in need of reinforcements.

At this critical juncture, a Persian nobleman with a black, glossy beard, a green tunic, and a distinctive high Persian cap arrived in Kandahar.

He introduced himself as Aga Khan, the spiritual leader of the Nizari Ismailis.

His arrival in Kandahar was fortuitous. With 200 horsemen at his disposal, he was just what the British needed. An alliance was swiftly formed. The British provided Aga Khan with food, shelter, and a monthly pension in exchange for his help in fighting against the Afghans…. his own *ummah* (community of Muslims).

In this way, Nizari Imam Aga Khan, once a fugitive, had now become a mercenary of infidels.

This event marks the beginning of the relationship between the Aga Khans and the British, a bond that continues to this day.

Aga Khan III, in his memoirs, affirms that his grandfather fought against his own people:

"In his wanderings over the next few years, my grandfather encountered and rendered significant assistance to the British in their military and imperial expansion northward and westward from the Punjab. In Sindh, he raised and maintained a troop of light cavalry, and during the latter stages of the First Afghan War, in 1841 and 1842, he and his cavalry supported General Nott in Kandahar and General England when he advanced from

Sindh to join Nott. For these services, and others he rendered to Sir Charles Napier during the conquest of Sindh in 1843-1844, my grandfather was granted a pension by the British Government."

Aga Khan in India

After completing his bloody assignment in Kandahar, Aga Khan was sent to Sindh with General England. In his work, *Administration of Sindh*, Sir William Napier describes Aga Khan's role in the conquest:

"Amongst those who provided secret information was the Persian Prince, Aga Khan, whose true title was the Emir of the Mountains. He was the lineal heir to the ancient Assassins. Although no longer the formidable figure who had once made kings tremble and armies quail, this wandering occult potentate still wielded considerable influence. His people, spread across Asia from the Indus to the Mediterranean, supplied him with both revenue and valuable intelligence. He had come to Sindh with a train of horsemen before the conquest, was aware of Ameer's plan to assault the Presidency, had protested it, and afterward provided crucial information that highlighted the dismal vanity of Outram's leadership. He and his horsemen fought alongside the British during the war. In return, he received

a pension from the Supreme Government, though his position and actions were regarded with suspicion. He was kept under surveillance and even prevented from leaving Sindh, where he intended to make a religious journey to Baghdad. Nevertheless, he maintained friendly relations with the General."

Due to the propagation activities of his ancestors over the past five centuries, Aga Khan already had a following in India. Upon completing his mission in Sindh, he arrived in Bombay in 1846 via Kutch. The prophecy of the Nizari Ismaili Pirs had come true.

Kalki had arrived!

The Aga Khan's arrival in India was a joyous occasion for the *Khojas* of Gujarat. After all, it marked their first meeting with the long-awaited *avatar* of lord Vishnu since the days of Pir Satgur Noor. But the celebrations didn't last long.

Soon, bloodshed marred the *Khoja* community.

Barbhayas (twelve brothers)

It may be recalled that Pir Shams back in the fourteenth century had given his Hindu converts a name….

Khoja. With time however, the Khoja community had split between Sunni and Shia persuasions.

In 1829, seventeen years before Aga khan arrived in India, a dispute had arisen within the *Khoja* community over the payment of *dasond.*

Some members of the *Khoja* community claimed to be Sunni Khojas and denied Aga Khan's authority. To resolve the issue, Aga khan had sent his grandmother, Marie Bibi, to Bombay. Marie, a powerful woman known for her excellent mediation skills, persuaded the rebels to resume the payment of *dasond.*

She, however, failed to convince twelve obstinate Sunni Khoja rebels who became known as the *barbhayas.*

Upon Aga Khan's arrival in Bombay in 1846, he began demanding religious dues and 'first insertion' rights, an ancient custom that involved the Imam having the right to sexual relations with every bride seeking his blessings.

The *Barbhayas* revolted against these demands. They were swiftly excommunicated.

This meant their community, friends and family would dissolve all ties with them, they would be banned from trading within the community and their dead bodies would not be given a space in Nizari burial ground.

A punishment that condemned them to a slow, lonely, and painful death!!

Soon after, a *barbhaya* Noor Mohammad Amersey was found dead under suspicious circumstances. However, what happened next horrified both the dissidents and the entire Bombay community.

Mahim Massacre

In those days, *Khojas* from both Sunni and Shia backgrounds gathered for their daily prayers at the Mahim *Jamatkhana* in Bombay. The Shia Khojas, followers of Aga Khan, worshipped on the ground floor, while the Sunni dissidents worshipped on the upper floor.

On 13 November 1850, twenty of Aga Khan's followers ambushed the Sunni dissidents and hacked three of them to death. The fourth died on the way to the hospital, while two others were severely wounded. The massacre took place in full view of the victims' families, including women and children.

To everyone's shock, the investigation authorities found that one of the swords used in the killings belonged to Aga Khan. The suspicion grew further when he canonized the perpetrators as martyrs in *Jamatkhana.*

Eventually, four of the perpetrators were brought to justice, but no charges were laid Aga Khan…. the British crony!!

The media began to smell a dead rat, which they found in the time to come!!

Treason Charges

Aga Khan's arrival in India might have been a joyous occasion for his followers. However, they were unaware that their Imam was not just a spiritual leader but also a rebel, a fugitive and a mercenary. A sword hung over his head for revolting against the Persian regime.

As expected, soon after his arrival in Bombay, the British received a request for his extradition to Persia to face treason charges.

The British, however, declined the request.

Although the British had saved his life, Aga Khan harbored resentment toward them. After all the British had declined his demands for a pension increase and honors given to most princes and chiefs in India.

To satisfy his desire for recognition, he devised a scheme.

His Highness

Aga khan's wife, Sarv-i-Jahan Khanum, being the daughter of His Majesty Fateh Ali Shah Qajar of Persia, was royal by birth.

Aga khan wondered, if she were in India, would she not be treated as royalty? More importantly, as her husband, would he not be treated accordingly?

He decided to reunite with his family who lived in Baghdad since his days as a rebel in Persia. In July 1853, Sarv-i-Jahan Khanum arrived in Bombay. One of her first tasks upon arrival was to write to Governor Lord Falkland:

"The inadequate pension of Rs 1000, which His Highness receives from your government, is supplemented by his other resources; even then, it is barely sufficient to meet his expenses. My resources have been usurped by those who, by the sword, claim superiority over such estates in Persia, and I now find myself in a foreign land, in a state of want, and unable to maintain myself in keeping with my rank... Several Persian refugees, though far inferior in rank

and position, have been generously provided for by your government and enjoy pensions. I trust I do not appeal in vain for suitable assistance from your lordship's Government."

The irony was glaring.

The Imam's wife addressed her husband as His Highness, claimed royal birth, and then, in the same breath, begged for money.

Regardless, Aga Khan plot worked!!

From that point on, the Bombay Government began referring to him as His Highness...though his request for a pension increase was still declined.

The Bookie

Now that his family had joined him, making ends meet became more of a struggle. This was despite the religious income from his followers in India and East Africa. Soon, he found an alternative source of income.

Aga Khan became a regular at the Bombay racecourse, making money as a bookie.

In his book, *The Shi'a of India*, author John Norman Hollister notes:

"He is slightly lame, wears a thin glossy black beard, and is perhaps the most assiduous frequenter of the

racecourse on the island. This man is no other than His Highness Aga Khan, a Persian refugee nobleman and high priest of the Khojahs... known at clubs, a patron of amusements, a giver and taker of odds on the racecourse, not unacquainted with the mysteries of betting books."

Death Threat

On 29 April 1861, Dharamsey Poonja, a dissident leader, received a death threat in a letter written in Gujarati. Poonja placed an ad in The Times of India, offering a reward of Rs 2,000 for any information that could lead to identifying the letter's author.

Robert Knight, a newspaper editor, was one of the few people who discovered Aga Khan's connection to the feared "assassins of Alamut." Convinced that Aga Khan was behind the death threat, Knight published an article recounting the history of the assassins.

"He is the open enemy of all improvement and progress in the cast because he is well-informed enough to know that his pretensions rest only upon the people's ignorance. There can be no peace for the Khoja tribe unless the Government banishes this man... Politically, it is a grave error to allow the residence of Aga Khan among a dense population of ignorant and fanatical Muslims, such as

surround us."

The article created a sensation not only in Bombay but throughout India. Whoever the author of the letter might have been, the incident invoked memories of the 1850 Mahim massacre. Fingers once again pointed at Aga Khan as the instigator. After all, he was the descendant of the dreaded assassins, and bloodshed had followed him since his arrival in Bombay.

Despite the accusations, Aga Khan honored Dharamsey Poonja with a shawl in public and laid the foundations for a mosque for the dissidents. This helped erase any doubts that he or his worshippers were involved in the scandal.

The community at large, however, described the ceremony as high-class hypocrisy.

On 21 November 1862, The Times of India published an article:

"The apathy with which the Government of this country sometimes tolerates the evil that admits to remedy, and a resort to which would be followed by great public benefit, receives a fair illustration in the continued tolerance of that mischievous imposter known amongst us as H.H. Aga Khan. How long, we inquire, are the educated and enlightened men of the Khoja community to submit to the

vulgar tyranny of this man? And to go in terror of their lives from the ignorant fanatics who are known to be at his bidding on this island, Bombay, and who ten years ago committed a wholesale massacre at Mahim on his behalf, if not (as is generally believed) at his instigation. In tolerating this man's presence here, the Government is doing all that lies in its power to keep the Khoja community steeped in ignorance and fanaticism, for which we shall perhaps someday pay dearly."

Supporting this article, another newspaper, The Poonah Observer, wrote:

"The Aga Khan is, after all, determined to prove antagonistic to the reforming party under Dharamsey Poonja. The Government should summarily deport this 'center of mischief,' as The Times of India recommended. His influence, as the prince of assassins, is extremely baneful in a civilized country, and the sooner he is taught to 'cool his heels,' the better for all."

The media and the Barbhayas joined calls for Agakhan's deportation…which never happened for obvious reasons.

Nevertheless, Aga Khan found himself at the center of a media storm, his connections and conduct under fierce scrutiny. To negotiate, Aga Khan compelled each of his disciples to sign a loyalty document. Those who refused to sign were condemned as rebels—excommunicated and left to endure a slow, agonizing death.

For the dissidents, this was the last straw!!

The Khoja Case

In 1866, the dissidents filed a case against Aga Khan in the Bombay High Court which became widely known as the Khoja Case.

The plaintiffs asserted that they were Sunni Muslims and, therefore, Aga Khan had no authority over them. They sought financial transparency, the right to elect their leadership, and a prohibition on Aga Khan from interfering in community matters particularly his powers to excommunicate *Khojas*, demand spiritual tributes, and claim the right of first insertion.

The defense attorneys countered that the *Khoja* community had a long history of loyalty to Aga Khan and his ancestors.

Regarding the plaintiffs' claim to be Sunni Muslims, they argued that these individuals were *"Hindus with a Muslim cultivation and Muslim development of their creed."*

To support this argument, *ginan Dasavatar* (The Ten Avatars) was presented as evidence, depicting Aga Khan's ancestor, Mawla Ali, as *Nakalanki,* the tenth *avatar* of Vishnu.

Justice Arnold ruled that all *Khojas,* including those who considered themselves Sunni Muslims, had the right to pray on the premises and use the property. However, he argued that the "original religion" of the *Khojas* would determine their identity and, consequently, their rightful leader.

After examining *Dasavatar,* he concluded that the *Khojas* were, in fact, Hindus rather than Muslims.

He also ruled that Aga Khan was the rightful leader because the majority of *Khojas* revered him as an incarnation of Vishnu. Thus, as a religious entity, Aga Khan had the right to collect religious tributes.

Although this judgment put out the immediate fire for Aga Khan, it irrevocably damaged his integrity.

Victory for Dissidents

Once again, in 1872, on the auspicious occasion of *Eid*, Aga Khan's worshippers barred the Sunni dissidents from entering the Jamatkhana to offer their prayers. The dissidents Khan Mohammad Habibbhoy, Peer Mohammad Kassambhoy, and Fazul Noormohammad filed a case in the court of law.

Mr. Macfarlane, the dissidents' counsel, argued that his clients had the same right to access *Jamatkhana* as the opposition. He reminded the court that the *Khoja Case* had already determined that all Khojas, whether Sunni or Shia, had the right to pray at the premises and use the property when needed.

Mr. Habibbhoy further alleged that Aga Khan had been collecting signatures of loyalty and threatening excommunication for those who declined to sign.

The Supreme Court ruled:

Aga Khan has failed to establish any right or ownership over the property of the caste or any authority to exclude individuals from the privileges of the caste. The Quran does not support the claim of such a right, nor does English Law.

Following this ruling, Aga Khan kept a low profile until he died in 1881. His tomb is located at Hassanabad in South Bombay.

Aga Khan II – Aqa Ali Shah

Upon Aga Khan's death, his eldest surviving son, Aqa Ali Shah, succeeded him as the forty-seventh Imam of the Nizari Isma'ili Muslims, adopting the title of Aga Khan II.

Agakhan II

Born in 1830 in Mahallat, Persia, during his father's tenure as Governor of Kerman province, Ali Shah was a mere boy of eight when he witnessed his father's rebellion against the Shah.

In 1840, he and his mother, Sarv-i-Jahan Khanum, were sent to the safety of neighboring Iraq. There, young Ali Shah lived with his mother for thirteen years, during which time he studied metaphysics and religious philosophy.

He would eventually reunite with his father in Bombay in 1853, as discussed.

During his Imamate, Aga Khan II maintained and strengthened his relationship with the British. His appointment to the Bombay Legislative Council was a testament to his capabilities and high standing.

Beyond his solid ties with the British, he also developed strong, cordial relations with the Indian community, earning the presidency of the Muhammadan National Association.

Aga Khan II was also renowned for his collection of the finest Arabian horses, his skill as an accomplished rider, and his fearlessness as a big-game hunter."

However, the Imam's personal life was marred by ongoing tragedies. He witnessed early deaths of two wives, his eldest son, Shihab al-Din Shah, died in his early thirties from cardiac arrest, while his second son, Nur al-Din Shah, tragically died in a riding accident at the age of twenty- three.

The Imam himself passed away in 1885 at the age of fifty-five, after a battle with pneumonia.

He left behind two survivors: his wife, Shams ul Mulk and his only surviving son, seven-and-a-half-year-old, Sultan Mohammad.

Lady Ali Shah

Shams ul-Mulk, also known as Lady Ali Shah, was the granddaughter of the Shah of Persia. In 1867, she married Aga Khan II, a nobleman, in Ispahan. The couple spent most of their married life in India.

Lady Aly Shah

Upon her husband's premature death, Lady Ali Shah assumed a crucial role in managing the Aga khan system until young Sultan Mohammad began to take on responsibilities as Imam.

A woman of distinction, Lady Ali Shah was celebrated not only for her intellect, but also for her talents as a poet, political strategist, shrewd investor, and passionate advocate of Sufi literature.

Her influence extended beyond the Nizari Ismaili community: during World War I, she played a vital part in galvanizing support for the British among influential Persians and raising funds for medical care for the injured.

Lady Ali Shah's contributions also reshaped the Nizari Ismaili community. After all it was her far sightedness that exposed her young son, Sultan Mohammad, the future Imam, to Western education rather than traditional Perso-Arabic schooling.

From this point forward, the Imams, their followers, and the Imamate began to embrace Western ideas and perspectives.

Accordingly, Sultan Mohammad, became the first in Nizari Ismaili Imam in history to adopt a Western attire, forgoing the traditional Perso-Arabic style and, notably, the iconic beard.

In 1937, Lady Ali Shah suffered a stroke, resulting

in cognitive loss. Sensing that her time was near, she left Pune for Baghdad, where she passed away in 1938. She was laid to rest beside her husband, Aga Khan II, in Najaf, Iraq.

Her only surviving son, Sultan Mohammad, the forty-eight Imam would usher in a new era for the Nizari Ismaili faith and community.

As Aga Khan III, he would transform the Nizari Ismailism into what I refer to as… *Agakhanism.*

Chapter 3

Aga Khan III – A Political Genius

Riches, politics, sex, lies, deceit, betrayal and greed.

The story of Aga Khan III, Sultan Mohammad Shah (SMS), the forty-eighth Imam of Nizari Ismaili Muslims, is full of these elements, making it feel more like a Hollywood blockbuster than a historical narrative.

When we look back at 1,300 years of Shia Ismaili history, only a few events stand out:

Mawla Ali's life, Imam Husayn's sacrifice, the rise of the Fatimid Caliphate in North Africa, the Nizari State in Persia, Pir Satgur Noor's Indian mission, and… SMS's long and dynamic Imamate.

As discussed, SMS, the Aga Khan III was the first Nizari Ismaili Imam to fully embrace a western lifestyle and thought!!

His relationship with the British was more than just a continuation of family ties; it drew him much closer to them than his ancestors had been. More significantly, this connection enabled him to carry the title of His Highness, a distinction previously held by his father and grandfather.

At just twenty years old, Queen Victoria honored him with the title of Knight Commander of the Indian Empire (KCIE). He would go on to receive numerous other prestigious decorations from British, Turkish, German, and Persian royalty.

Agakhan III

On a personal note, SMS married four times and became known for rubbing shoulders with royalty and high society.

In addition to his social and political achievements, SMS played a pivotal role in the creation of Pakistan, a contribution he detailed in his book, *India in Transition*.

As a Nizari Ismaili Imam, he was the first to formally constitutionalize the community and establish institutions focused on education, social welfare, and economic development, all while placing a strong emphasis on educating girls.

But above all, the crowning achievement of his Imamate was transforming Nizarism into Agakhanism, a social club with a religious frontage.

A 'club' unlike any other, the cult catapulted him into becoming one of the wealthiest men of his time."

SMS was undoubtedly a towering figure, a rich celebrity, a statesman albeit without a state, a horse breeder, an author, a Shia Imam, and, to millions, a living deity.

However, his brilliance was tainted by a willingness to deceive those who trusted and revered him.

SMS was born on 2 November 1877 in Karachi. He was the only surviving child of the forty-seventh Nizari Imam, Shah Ali Shah (Aga Khan II), and Lady Ali Shah.

Survive he did but just.

Doctors were doubtful about the infant's chances of survival. Yet against all odds, he lived for nearly eighty years, of which seventy-one were spent as an Imam.

Upon his father's death in 1885, the seven-and-a-half-year-old boy inherited the Imamate, becoming the forty-eighth Imam of the Nizari Ismailis.

The British Spy

In 1898, still in his early twenties, SMS traveled to Europe. There, he was captivated, especially by the allure of white European women, whom he found far more attractive than the dutiful Indian wives. More than that, he relished the admiration and respect he received from Europeans, a stark contrast to the reverence of his *Khoja* followers, who saw him as a divine figure.

The Duke of Connaught, Queen Victoria's son, who had known SMS from Bombay, introduced him to the high society of London. This connection led to the distinguished honor of being named a Knight Commander of the Indian Empire (KCIE).

But why was SMS given such an honorific title?

After all, at twenty, he had no significant service record to the Crown. Marco van Grondelle, in his thesis *Across the Threshold of Modernity*, provides an answer:

"The Aga Khan gained temporal status, and Britain gained a friend who was well-disposed towards the Empire. The Aga Khan gained a high degree of control over his movement. Britain gained a worldwide network. The Aga Khan became a statesman. Britain gained a valuable set of eyes and ears in the Muslim world."

But why, one might wonder, did the British need a spy in the Muslim world?

For three centuries, Britain had successfully ruled vast territories across the globe with their policy of *"divide and rule,"* including India.

In the wake of the 1857 rebellion, unrest simmered throughout the empire, with Indian nationalist sentiment growing ever stronger, fueling rising demands for independence."

If that wasn't enough, Britain's participation in the two World Wars drained the British treasury. Particularly after the Second World War, the British began counting their days in India.

However, maintaining a presence in the subcontinent, particularly in the northwest of India, was crucial to British foreign policy. This was primarily due to trade routes and the need to monitor Russian activities in the region.

The northwest of British India, as it is now, had a Muslim majority, and to win their support, the British sought a Muslim figure who could relate to their concerns and priorities, particularly from an Islamic perspective. After all, if anything could sway the Muslims, it was their faith.

SMS was the perfect candidate for this role. As a young, educated Muslim, he was multilingual, well-connected, well-spoken, intelligent, and, most importantly, driven by ambition.

He seized the opportunity with both hands.

Reflecting on his loyalty to the British during World War I, he confirmed his commitment in his memoirs:

"By the time I reached Zanzibar, the situation had become critical. In the last days of July and the first days of August, there was an exchange of increasingly urgent telegrams. Russia and Germany were at war; the Germans had invaded Belgium; and on August 4th, Britain declared

war on Germany. I had no hesitations, no irresolution. My ambitions, aspirations, hopes, and interests all narrowed to one or two intensely personal decisions. I had one overriding emotion to go to England as fast as I could and offer my services in whatever capacity they could best be used. I was in good health, still young and strong; my place was with the British."

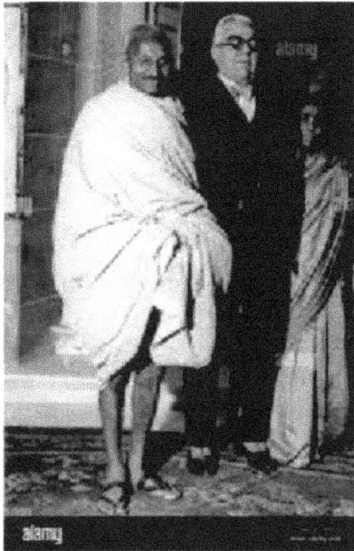

SMS with Mahatma Gandhi and Sarojini Naidu

He then went on to call on Lord Kitchener, the Secretary of State for War, with whom he had long been acquainted from his time in India.

Having served together on the Viceroy's Legislative Council for more than a decade,

SMS urged Kitchener that he be enlisted as a private in the Indian contingent heading to the Western Front.

Although he was not enlisted as a private, SMS's first covert assignment came soon after.

The competition between Britain and Russia for influence over Afghanistan had been ongoing since his grandfather's era. SMS instructed his followers in neighboring Northwest Frontier of undivided India to monitor Russian activities.

Soon SMS was appointed a Grand Commander of the Indian Empire (GCIE), further solidifying his role as a key ally to the British. It became increasingly clear with time that he was acting as a tool for British interests.

The Pakistan Movement

Syed Ahmad Khan was an Indian Muslim reformer, lawyer, and philosopher, who had adopted a Western outlook and thinking. At the dawn of the nineteenth century, he entered the service of the East India Company and remained loyal to the British Raj.

Initially, he advocated for Hindu-Muslim unity, but a shift occurred when a linguistic issue changed his views.

The language spoken by most Indians was Hindi but owing to the Mughal influence, Persian had been the official language of the northern regions of British India.

Having exterminated the Mughals, the British Government decided to replace Persian with a local vernacular.

However, instead of choosing Hindi, the most widely spoken language, they opted for Urdu— a language spoken by a minority, predominantly Muslims.

This created a significant advantage for Urdu-speaking students when applying for government jobs, to the dismay of the majority Hindu population.

Soon the issue assumed a communal form. Witnessing the strife, Sir Syed, now disillusioned, came to believe that Hindus and Muslims did not share common values, morals, or beliefs, and, therefore, could not coexist.

Tragically, this sentiment developed roots among the Muslim population, setting the stage for future divisive and horrific events.

Some argue that the British deliberately engineered this linguistic issue to drive a wedge between Hindus and Muslims, and Sir Syed had obliged.

Regardless, a two-nation theory had emerged. In 1875, Sir Syed took a significant step toward fostering separation by founding a Muslim college in Aligarh, northern India.

Over time, the British and their allies, including SMS, carefully nurtured this seed of discord.

In 1902, Lord Curzon held the Durbar in Delhi to celebrate King Edward VII's and Queen Alexandra's ascension as Emperor and Empress of India.

During his visit, Lord Curzon also convened an educational conference and put twenty-five-year-old SMS behind the microphone.

While he did discuss education, his focus was specifically on the needs of Muslims rather than the Indian population at large. Moreover, he used the platform to advocate for Aligarh College to become a Muslim university.

Speaking on the occasion, he said:

"If we are truly earnest in deploring the fallen condition of our people, we must unite in an effort for their redemption. First and foremost, we must now focus on

establishing a university where Muslim youth can receive not only modern sciences but also a deeper understanding of their glorious past and religion. The atmosphere of such an institution, being a residential university like Oxford, should give more attention to character than to mere examinations. Muslims in India have legitimate interests in the intellectual development of their co-religionists in Turkey, Persia, Afghanistan, and elsewhere. The best way to support them is by making Aligarh a Muslim Oxford. We are confident that by founding this university, we can arrest the decline of Islam. If we are not willing to make sacrifices for such a cause, must I not conclude that we do not truly care whether Islam endures or not? We want Aligarh to be a center of learning that commands the same respect as Berlin, Oxford, Leipzig, or Paris. We aim to revitalize branches of Muslim learning that are rapidly fading and add them to the global pool of knowledge."

The speech, focusing on the creation of a Muslim university, urged Muslims to unite and advocate for Islam.

The so-called education conference had drawn a religious line in the sand mobilizing the British policy of Divide and Rule.

That same year, SMS also chaired the Central Foundation Committee of the proposed Muslim University, alongside Secretary Maulana Shaukat and other prominent Muslim leaders. He contributed Rs 100,000, an annual grant of Rs 10,000, and helped raise an additional Rs 2.6 million for the Muslim cause.

His efforts earned him the first honorary presidency of the All-India Muslim League when it was formed in Dhaka in 1906.

Soon, SMS led a delegation to present Muslim concerns to the British Viceroy in Simla. The delegation argued that Muslims were being discriminated against and ill-treated, demanding more political representation and special treatment.

The British, ever adept at appeasing potential unrest, 'obliged.'

As a result, SMS gained significant leverage. His passion for Aligarh Muslim University, combined with his leadership of the Simla delegation, positioned him as the 'voice of Muslims.'

However, what the Muslim community failed to realize

was that they were being led down a path of bloodshed and devastation.

In 1920, Aligarh Muslim University was officially established, with SMS as its pro-chancellor. True to form, politics soon entered the campus with the creation of the All-India Muslim Students Federation (AIMSF). It was an open secret that the federation had ties to the All-India Muslim League (AIML) and its divisive policies.

Over time, Aligarh University became a center for the Pakistan Movement.

In his memoirs, SMS expressed his pride in the role Muslims played in the university's creation:

"We may claim with pride that Aligarh was the product of our efforts and no outside benevolence. Surely, it may also be claimed that the independent sovereign nation of Pakistan was born in the Muslim University of Aligarh."

Eventually, in 1947, the British and the AIML achieved their goal. India was partitioned and Pakistan became a reality. Following the partition, SMS once commented on Karachi, the economic hub of Pakistan, saying,

'It will one day become Paris.'

However, time proved the so-called all-knowing wrong!

The creation of Pakistan led to riots which killed

million innocent people, including Muslims. Moreover, it left a legacy of ongoing conflict, wars and terrorism.

The republic of Pakistan proved to be dysfunctional and the time of writing on the verge of collapse.

Devout but gullible Muslims were betrayed—not only by the British but their leaders including Sir Syed, SMS, Allama Iqbal, and Qaid-e-Azam Mohammad Ali Jinnah.

World War I

In the early twentieth century, the clouds of war gathered over Europe. Britain, France, and Russia formed the Triple Entente, countering the imperialistic ambitions of Germany, who allied with Austria-Hungary, and Italy. They formed what became known as the Triple Alliance.

Due to its strategic location, securing Turkey's loyalty was vital for both alliances. However, Turkey sided with the Triple Alliance, largely due to the strong ties between Germany and Turkey established by German Chancellor Kaiser Wilhelm II.

London was concerned…not necessarily because of Turkey's military strength, but due to the influence of the Ottoman Caliph over Muslims worldwide, many of whom resided in British colonies. If the Caliph was to encourage

Muslims to rise against the British, it could threaten Britain's war efforts.

Therefore, London needed to secure Muslim loyalty. Coincidentally, SMS delivered a speech in India that denounced the Islamic Caliphate.

In his address, the SMS declared:

"Let there be no misunderstanding of the real attitude of the Indian Muslim towards Turkey. There is much discussion in Europe regarding the Sultan's role as Khalif. The Indian Muslim does not recognize the Sultan as Khalif and offers him no allegiance in that capacity. However, he does regard Turkey as the embodiment of the temporal power of Islam. The events of the last two years have not shaken the Indian Muslim's belief that, in her own interest, Great Britain should support the Ottoman power. The Indian Muslim does not ask for the surrender of British interests, he simply points out that these interests align with Muslim sentiments and wishes."

Following the outbreak of the war, Indian Muslims fought for Britain, contributing to the victory of the Triple Entente and hence the British.

Fallout with the British

Triple Entente victory in World War I was no cause for SMS to celebrate.

Coincidently, from that moment on, the British attitude toward SMS began to shift.

He was going out of favor!!

In 1924, the Indian Legislative Council passed a resolution nominating SMS for the Nobel Peace Prize in recognition of his 'strenuous, persistent, and successful efforts' to maintain peace between Turkey and the Western Powers.

The resolution was sent to London for approval before being forwarded to the Nobel committee in Norway. But the nomination met a significant setback in London, where Sir Arthur Hertzel, the Under Secretary of State, rejected it outright.

His letter stated:

"I have the lowest possible opinion of the Aga Khan, both as a man, as a religious leader (save the mark), and as a politician. As a politician, he is an opportunist, plain and simple, always eager to align with whichever side he believes will prevail. He is seldom honest enough to do the hard work for the government in obscurity or unpopularity. During the war, he did nothing of note except issue a proclamation. While it was undoubtedly useful, his loyalty to the Khojas would likely not have been a significant asset if

there had been serious trouble in the Muslim world. His activities on the continent were largely private and mostly concerned with his own pleasures."

"I watched him closely, but the result confirmed only one thing: he is an easy-going voluptuary, content to pay for a quiet life. The Aga Khan had considerable influence with Mr. Montagu and used it to secure easier terms for Turkey during the negotiations again, a maneuver to restore his waning prestige in the Indian Muslim world. If the Nobel Prize is to be awarded on such grounds, I would argue that Mr. Montagu has far greater claims."

Ultimately, SMS was not nominated for the Nobel Peace Prize.

Having deluded himself of his lineage to the Fatimid Caliphs SMS, harbored ambitions of ruling over his own domain.

In 1933, he made a desperate appeal to Viceroy Willingdon, imploring for a territory—any territory—to rule.

His plea read:

"I beg to submit for your consideration my memorial, praying that my status as a ruling prince of the first class in the Bombay constituency be regularized, with the grant of some territory over which I may hold ruling powers. This

would allow my heirs and successors to enjoy a permanent, influential status in India, consistent with the prestige and dignity of my ancient lineage, as well as with the family traditions of loyal and devoted service to the British crown."

When Willingdon ignored his request, an audacious SMS next wrote to Sir Samuel Hoare, the Secretary of State for India:

"I leave the fate and future of my house in the hands of the highest authorities of the empire, to be decided as they think fair, just, and above all, in the interests of Great Britain, which has always been served so devotedly by myself and my predecessors.

This time the appeal was formally declined. SMS reflected on the rejection in his memoirs:

"Some busybodies have ferreted out the fact that in the 1930s, I approached the Government of India and suggested that I might be given a territorial state and join the company of ruling princes. From the refusal of this request, they have drawn the erroneous and absurd conclusion that I was offended, and that in resentment, I abandoned all the principles and ideals I had cherished throughout my life. Nothing could be further from the truth. This is what really happened: it had long been felt among

the Ismaili community that it would be desirable to possess nal home not a large, powerful state, but something along the lines of Tangier or the Vatican a small piece of land that Ismailis from all over the world could call their own, where they could practice all their customs, establish their own laws, and, on the material side, build a financial center, complete with banks, investment trusts, insurance schemes, and welfare and provident arrangements. The idea of a territorial state made no appeal to me. However, given the strength of Ismaili sentiment on the matter, I approached the Government of India. For reasons I am sure were just and fair, the Government could not see their way of granting our request. The notion that they disapproved of me for making the request, or that I was hurt and disappointed by their refusal, is fantastic."

It is remarkable how SMS's perspective evolved between his appeal to Viceroy Willingdon and his depiction of it in his memoir.

To Willingdon, he had sought land for his heirs, but in his memoir, the land was intended for his followers!!

Later a significant rift developed between SMS and the local authorities in Zanzibar over the Nizari burial grounds. Discontented, SMS appealed to the British

Government for intervention. However, they refused, advising him to resolve the matter with the local authorities directly. Frustrated by the British India Office's indifference, SMS expressed his bitterness in the memoirs:

"I can assure you that nothing will hurt British prestige throughout the East more than discourteous methods in East Africa. The enemies of England (who, for that reason alone, are my enemies as well) will point to the case of the Aga Khan and say: 'Look at how the British treat their loyal servants. After seventy years of devoted service, the moment he and his followers are no longer of direct use, they are not only cast aside but kicked to the curb by British authorities. And that is all one can expect when their utility has waned.'"

Nazi Connections

After the British abandoned him, SMS decided to reciprocate. During the Second World War, he began to appease the Nazis. In 1938, he wrote an article for the Anglo-German newspaper, *Review "Why I Consider Hitler a Pillar of Peace?"*

However, the very next year, SMS's words exploded in his face!

Hitler invaded Poland, marking the beginning of horrors that would follow. He next set his sights on France, where SMS was living with his family at the time.

In a panic, SMS fled for the safety of neutral Switzerland. There, he met an old German acquaintance, Prince Max von Hohenlohe-Ladenburg, and allegedly sent a message to Hitler through him:

"If he (Hitler) were planning to take over India, I would be happy to help organize the country."

Hitler ignored SMS's offer!

However, the following year, a news article in the London Sunday Pictorial strained his already fraught relationship with the British.

The headline read,

Is She to Blame? with a picture of SMS's second wife, Begum Andree Aga Khan, beneath it.

The article read:

"The leader of 10,000,000 Muslims, and once one of the wealthiest men in the world, is in Paris. Why? Since the fall of France, the Aga Khan has been living with his beautiful French wife and their eight-year-old son in Switzerland. He has been cut off from his vast riches. A report reaching London last night says that the Aga Khan traveled from Switzerland at the invitation of Hitler."

Upon reading the report, SMS vehemently denied any involvement with Hitler. However, the India Office in London was not convinced. They were increasingly concerned about his intentions, activities, and pretensions. They issued a press release:

"We do not believe that he would accept an invitation from the Germans to return to Paris, though it is possible that his wife may have influenced him. Meanwhile, the Aga Khan's house in Paris has become the meeting place of Nazis. Sumptuous dinner parties are being held for Hitler's friends, but the name of the host remains unknown."

Though the British were unsure about the Nazi invitation, post-World War II SMS was caught red-handed.!!

A treasonous memo, addressed to the Nazi Party in 1942, was discovered by the Allies at the close of the war.

In it, SMS wrote:

"If you give me ten to fifteen days' warning, I will have for you 30,000 armed Arabs, among my most faithful disciples, who will shoot the Gaullistes (the French) in the back."

Since France was a British ally, the memo was damning enough to prove treason…punishable by death. However, to SMS's good fortune, the British decided against prosecuting him, for reasons that remain undisclosed.

A Muslim 'Roll' Model

O believers, wine and gambling, idols, and divining arrows are an abhorrence, the work of Satan. So, keep away from it, that you may prevail. Satan only desires to arouse discord and hatred among you with wine and gambling and to deter you from the mention of God and prayer. Will you desist?

Qur'an, Sura Al-Ma'ida Ayat 90-91

SMS was not just an ordinary Muslim; he was a Shia Imam, a divine representative, a sacred guide, and, in many ways, an Islamic role model. However, his conduct and indiscretions not only contradicted his mandate but also became an affront to all Muslims.

His memoirs confirm that he gambled, a *haram* (forbidden) act in Sharia law.

A few weeks later, I went to the Derby; I had a small bet of a sovereign at sixty-six to one on a horse called Jeddah.

Looking back on my memories of owning, breeding, and racing horses, I do not propose to give a detailed account of my wins, my prizes, my bloodstock sales, and so forth...

Though gambling was considered a grave sin, it paled in comparison to one even more severe in Islam…adultery, a transgression punishable by stoning to death.

Elsa Maxwell, an American socialite and film producer who knew SMS closely, once said:

"No one was a greater coureur (woman chaser) than Aga. He had many mistresses. He made love to many women, important women in England, great big names."

SMS's Women

Shahzadi

In his youth, SMS became infatuated with Shahzadi, his beautiful cousin, daughter of his paternal uncle, Aga Jungi Shah, who disapproved of the marriage proposal.

Coincidentally, Jungi Shah was murdered in Jeddah while returning from *hajj* (the holy pilgrimage). Though fingers were pointed at SMS, his involvement was never proven. Eventually, his mother Lady Ali Shah ensured her son's wish was fulfilled.

The couple tied the knot in Pune. Tragically for Shahzadi, SMS's infatuation soon began to fade. He realized that they were fundamentally different people: he was Western in thought and outlook, while Shahzadi adhered to a more conservative Muslim culture.

SMS began spending time away from her and eventually stopped visiting her.

After a few years of marrying SMS, Shahzadi died…lonely, resentful and heartbroken!!

She was thirty-eight!!

Theresa

Monaco, a city on the southeast coast of France, has long been a playground for the rich and famous. Monte Carlo, its entertainment precinct, is renowned for its casinos, film festivals, ballet, and vibrant nightlife.

During one such visit to a ballet performance in Monte Carlo, thirty-four-year-old SMS fell in love with a nineteen-year-old Italian ballerina, Theresa Magliano.

Gina Lamy, Theresa's co-dancer, later recounted the Story:

Aga was a regular at ballet performances. One day, after a performance, when we were resting outside the hall, a journalist approached Theresa. She was told that a very rich man loved her and would like to meet her the next day.

Theresa, who was from a humble background, seized this once-in-a-lifetime opportunity to go out with a rich celebrity. She understood SMS sought physical intimacy rather than marriage, at least at that stage.

Their adulterous relationship produced two sons. Sadly, the firstborn, Giuseppe Mahdi, died of meningitis in infancy. The second, Aly Salomone Khan, survived.

In the summer of 1911, when Aly was born in Turin, Italy, SMS was in London, celebrating King George's coronation. It was here that he first heard of Aly's birth, but before meeting his newborn, he had several political matters to attend to. One of them was delivering a lecture on the Muslim condition!!

SMS with Theresa and baby Guiseppe

SMS would not meet Aly until a month later!!

It was no surprise that Aly never bonded with SMS throughout his life. Worse still, Aly would face a disturbing emotional issue as an adult.

He was the result of an illegitimate relationship!!

This dilemma began with his birth certificate, which is still on file in the town hall of Turin, Italy.

The certificate, dated June 17, 1911, reads:

In the year 1911, 17th of June, 5 pm, before me, Piere Carossa, acting vice secretary of the delegation (appointed December 31, 1909), officer of the civil government of Turin, has come Dr. Alfredo Pozzi, 39 years old, obstetrician, living in Turin, who declared that on June 13th, at 2 pm, in this house at 17 Corso Oporto, from the union of Teresa Magliano, unmarried, 22 years old, living on independent means, and His Highness The Aga Khan, son of the late Aga Ali Shah, 34 years old, born in Karachi (British India), living in Monte Carlo, was born a male child, who is not present and to whom the name Aly Salomone is given. Present as witnesses were Francesca Crescio, 28, living independent means, both residents of Turin. The child has not been shown owing to hygienic reasons.

Rumors of SMS's immorality soon began to spread throughout the Ismaili Nizari community and the broader Islamic world. However, SMS managed to convince them that he had married Theresa according to Muslim law in Cairo.

He confirmed this in his memoirs:

In 1908, this affection found a personal focus. I made the acquaintance of Mlle. Theresa Magliano, one of the most promising young dancers of the Ballet Opéra of Monte Carlo, a ballerina who in the opinion of the teachers of both the Paris Opéra and La Scala in Milan was assured of a brilliant future in her profession. She was then just nineteen. We fell deeply in love. In the spring of that year, she accompanied me to Egypt, and we were married in Cairo by Muslim law.

However, the master of deception was careful not to mention that it was a *Muta'h* (temporary marriage) ceremony.

Muta'h is a pre-Islamic Arabian tradition that allowed temporary marriage contracts with women while away from home. In modern times, *Muta'h* is widely regarded within the Islamic community as legal prostitution. The fact that SMS had married Theresa under a *Muta'h* contract was later confirmed in his will which was read out after he died in Geneva in 1957.

SMS eventually married Theresa in 1922, when Aly was eleven.

However, this did not mean that SMS would live with his family afterward. Instead, he bought them an apartment in Nice, France, and then left to pursue his *'other interests.'*

An excerpt from SMS's memoirs confirms this:

My wife lived largely in France. In 1909, my first son was born to her, whom I named Mehdi. His brief life ended in February 1911, and my second son, Aly, was born the following June. His birth brought profound solace and joy to my wife and me, but for her, the happiness of his babyhood was tinged with a solemn sense of responsibility. Long years had passed since there had been a son in our family, and the grief we felt at the loss of our firstborn gave a special sharpness and watchfulness to the care we exercised over his brother's upbringing. When he was quite little, he was pronounced delicate; one of the leading child specialists of the time believed in the health-giving properties of the Normandy coast, especially the sea air and bathing. From the time he was two or three, therefore, my wife took him each summer to Deauville, and their winters they spent in the south of France. For some years, my wife lived in Monte Carlo, and then she moved to Cimiez.

There were times when SMS was in Nice but did not stay with his young family. He preferred the luxury of Hotel Negresco, just a few miles away.

However, he did visit the family once a year, and being a wealthy man, he always brought numerous and expensive presents for his wife and son.

Theresa on the other hand, showered Aly with pure maternal love. As a result, Aly held his mother in deep reverence throughout his life.

Sadly, Theresa passed away of loneliness and resentment at just thirty-seven years old.... just like Shahzadi back in India.

The dream she cherished of building a family was never realized."

Tamara

The next woman in SMS's life was Tamara Karsaniva, a twenty-four-year-old, stunningly beautiful Russian ballerina. She performed with the famous Sergei Diaghilev's ballet company in Monte Carlo.

History seemed intent on repeating itself when SMS was drawn to Tamara in circumstances strikingly like those with Theresa.

However, the "I am rich" charm that worked with Theresa failed with Tamara. In addition to her extraordinary beauty, she possessed a high moral character. SMS hosted lavish parties, inviting Tamara to dance, but he could not entice her to his bed.

Instead, he found Josefina Kohalevska, a pretty dancer, far more obliging.

Andrée

Aix-les-Bains, France, was a familiar place for SMS. It was here that, in 1926, following Theresa's death, SMS ran into *Andrée Carron,* a dressmaker.

He had known her family for over a decade. *Andrée* came from humble circumstances, was undemanding, and, unlike other women in his life, was unlikely to interfere with his preferred lifestyle away from home.

SMS with Andree

He decided to marry her!

Despite being twenty years younger, *Andrée* agreed, likely influenced by SMS's fame and wealth. However, their religiosity became an obstacle.

He was a Muslim Imam, and *Andrée* was a Roman Catholic. Her devoutly Christian family insisted that they marry according to strict Christian traditions and that SMS would not pressure her into converting to Islam after the wedding. Even if SMS had agreed, such an undertaking would have been a challenging one for his followers.

Eventually, her family relented, and on 9 December 1929, a civil ceremony was followed by a brief Islamic one at the Aix-les-Bains town hall.

Apart from religious concerns, marriage faced another vexing issue…Aly. Accepting any woman other than Theresa as his mother was utterly unacceptable to him.

This was due not only to Theresa's nurturing love and care, but also because his father had deprived her of the fulfillment that comes with a conventional marriage.

However, over time, Andrée earned his affection. Four years later, Aly gained a stepbrother, Sadruddin, affectionately known as Sadri.

Unfortunately, for Andrée, her marriage to SMS was far from the "till death do us part" affair she might have hoped for.

In 1938, at sixty, SMS's male hormones kicked in… once again!!

Yvette

This time, the aging Imam fell for Yvette Blanche Labrousse, a former Miss France, who was half his age and six inches taller. After six years of extramarital affairs, it was time to divorce Andrée.

Yvette became his first wife to convert to Islam, accompanied him to, both social and religious functions, and importantly was his last wife.

SMS with Yvettte Labrousse

Divinity

Traditionally, Nizari Ismaili Imams had claimed divinity albeit implicitly.

But then came SMS, who for the first time in Nizari Ismaili history, declared himself...God!!

During a visit to Vadi Jamatkhana in South Bombay in 1902, SMS made an unprecedented declaration of divinity.

"There is no one greater than me. If you think of God, it is me. If you think of Pir, then too, it is me. If you think of Imam, it is also me!"

Over time, the divinity myth propagated within the guarded confines of *Jamatkhana* crystallized into undeniable truths for the faithful.

The followers began weaving stories about SMS's supernatural powers!!

What began as controlled storytelling evolved into an intricate web of glorification, manufacturing an entire mythology around the Imam. It's no surprise, then, that fakelore, though unofficial, is a fundamental pillar of *'Agakhanism.'* Passed down through generations via word-of-mouth, these narratives endure.

The Giver of Life

The *Deedar,* the act of physically seeing the Imam is the most anticipated and joyous occasion for an Aga Khan devotee. After all, in their eyes, God himself manifests before his creation.

In 1939, thousands of SMS followers gathered at *Hasanabad Jamatkhana* in South Bombay, eager for a glimpse of the celestial being. The crowd was already ecstatic, but to heighten the euphoria, a missionary was deployed to captivate and hypnotize them.

As the eager crowd waited for the divine arrival, the missionary began narrating the story of *Meraj,* the Prophet's mystical journey to meet God in heaven.

According to belief, when the Prophet reached the seventh sky and stood before the Divine, only God's hand emerged from behind the veil. One of the fingers flaunted a ring which Shia Muslims believe, belonged to Mawla Ali.

At that precise moment in the sermon, SMS's motorcade arrived. The missionary abruptly fell silent. As if in a trance, the congregation erupted into chants of *Salwat:*

"Allahumma s a l l i 'ala M u h a m m a d w a āli Muhammad."

"O Allah, let thy peace be on Prophet Muhammad and his progeny" a phrase implicitly directed at SMS himself.

SMS entered the compound, blessing his disciples as he made his way to his seat near the mausoleum of his grandfather, Aga Khan I.

Once settled, he summoned the missionary who had been stirring the crowd with the story of *Meraj*. With his gaze lowered and hands joined in submission; the missionary presented himself before the divine.

"What was the topic of your *waez*, missionary?" SMS asked.

"*Meraj, Khudawind*," the missionary replied.

"At what point did you discontinue the narration?" SMS inquired.

"I was at the moment when the Prophet saw a hand emerging from behind the curtain..." the missionary answered hesitantly.

SMS raised his right hand and, with divine authority, proclaimed:

"Do you know whose hand that was? It was this hand... this very hand!"

The fakelore continues...

Among the sea of devotees stood a single mother, a woman who had journeyed thousands of miles from Punjab to the megapolis of Bombay for a single glimpse of SMS, the divine.

Cradled in her arms was her six-month-old infant, whom she nursed as she awaited *Deedar*. But as fate would have it, the child developed a high fever. She considered leaving, searching for a doctor, but how could she? The ground was packed so tightly with bodies that moving seemed impossible. Even if she managed to push through the crowd, where would she find medical help in an unfamiliar city?

More importantly how could she abandon a once-in-a-lifetime opportunity to stand before God himself?

She decided to stay put... whispering to herself.

My Mawla is all-knowing and all-powerful. Would he not protect my child?

Then she began praying with her eyes closed.... lost in a trance!

When she regained consciousness, she was horror-struck!!

The infant had stopped breathing!!

Panic surged through her as she shook the child, hoping for a sign of life.

Nothing!!

His tiny body remained limp…. his breath gone!

Overcome with grief, she began chanting:

"Ya Ali Madad! O Ali, help!"

At that precise moment, amid the thousands gathered in the congregation, SMS turned to the *Mukhi* and commanded, *"Bring that woman to me."*

Volunteers pushed through the crowd, escorting her to the throne. Trembling, she stood before the divine, her lifeless child still in her arms.

SMS rose from his seat. He reached out, his hand resting on the baby's body. Then, with a commanding voice, he instructed the mother:

"Say '*Haizinda.*'" (The Imam is ever-present)

The woman's voice wavered *"Haizinda!"*

"Now say '*Kayam Paya.*'" (We have him forever)

"*Kayam Paya!" she mumbled.*

A heartbeat later, the baby's eyes flew open, and his cry filled the surrounding air.

The mother was ecstatic, and the crowd gasped. Their Imam had performed a *Mojiza*, a miracle!!

Their faith had been reaffirmed!

All lived happily ever after… all but the Khoja dissidents."

The Khoja Dissidents

During his time, SMS's grandfather, Aga Khan I, had faced a rebellion from Khoja dissidents. Though the dissent had simmered down after his death, it was far from extinguished.

The ghost of defiance returned…this time in response to SMS's extravagance. A band of rebels, led by the dissident Karim Ghulamali, openly protested SMS's extended absences in Europe, his extravagant lifestyle, his unyielding financial demands, and the doctrine that elevated him to the seat of God.

In a letter addressed directly to SMS, Ghulamali wrote:

"The Muslim Zakat is a voluntary contribution enjoined in the Holy Koran to be given in the name of God to the poor, the needy, the wayfarer. Yet, our impoverished brethren are compelled to surrender nearly 50% of their incomes in various forms not to God, but to Your Highness, who claims to be His earthly manifestation."

"These exactions are paid in money and in kind. From Karachi alone, there is a regular monthly contribution of Rs 20,000, not to mention the levies extracted from other regions. Beyond these steady tributes, there is a periodic drain of immense sums of money, jewelry, apparel, and other costly offerings whenever Your Highness graces us with a visit."

"In 1920, Your Highness visited Karachi and, after a stay of just 26 days, carried away Rs 15,000,000. Merely two years later, when Your Highness visited His Royal Highness, The Prince of Wales, in March 1922, our brethren contributed no less than Rs 154,000 despite the fact that Your Highness was among them for barely two hours."

When his submission was ignored, Ghulamali took matters into his own hands, distributing pamphlets throughout Karachi's Muslim community to raise awareness.

The content of these pamphlets stirred concern, particularly within SMS's inner circle. Alarmed by the potential repercussions, Lady Aly Shah, SMS's mother and trusted business advisor quickly intervened, writing to the Governor with an urgent appeal. She wrote:

The pamphlet is likely to cause tensions between different Islamic sects, and there is no doubt that it will incite hatred and contempt against the Ismailis, particularly among the illiterate class. If this highly objectionable pamphlet is not immediately suppressed, the consequences could be dangerous. The offensive nature of this publication is clear, and the law governing such matters must be enforced to ensure its proscription, which is necessary.

Lady Aly Shah's concern was met with a measured but dismissive response from the Governor, who refused to take any formal action. His reply, though diplomatic, made it clear that he saw no real threat in Ghulamali's pamphlet:

I am not suggesting that there is any truth whatsoever in the argument that abuse exists... and I can only regret that, under the circumstances as they have been put before me, the Government cannot proscribe the pamphlet. I am, however, fully confident that practically anyone who sees it will take the same action I did when it was sent to me and confine it to the only place for which it fits, namely, the wastepaper basket.

The Governor's apathy signaled a lack of urgency, dismissing Lady Aly Shah's fears and leaving the matter unresolved.

Haji Bibi Case

In 1896, during a *farman,* SMS made a proclamation that reinforced his image as a spiritual leader above worldly concern:

I don't seek your life nor your money, all I ask for is your heart. Your heart on your faith, that's all I ask for.

The believers took his words at face value, trusting in his sincerity. Little did they know that a legal battle involving their Imam would expose a very different reality.

In 1908, SMS found himself in the Bombay High Court when Haji Bibi, his cousin and the great-granddaughter of Aga Khan I, filed a lawsuit against him.

At the heart of the dispute was the inheritance of the estate of Aga Khan I. Traditionally, the Aga Khans had shared their wealth and religious income with their extended family. SMS's father, Aqa Ali Shah (Aga Khan II), had upheld this practice.

But SMS had broken with tradition, refusing to share

and keeping the estate under his sole control. The case threatened to expose not only his financial dealings but also the widening rift within his own family.

Haji Bibi, along with a few other family members, laid claim to a share of Aga Khan I's inheritance, arguing that their lineage followed the *Ithna'ashariyya* (Twelver) tradition of Islam. Under Islamic law, they insisted, they were entitled to a portion of the estate.

The case, reminiscent of the Khoja Case back in 1866, forced the court to examine both Islamic tenets and the religious customs of the *Khoja* community, including their practice of *ginans*.

After careful deliberation, Justice Russel delivered a verdict that would have lasting implications.

He ruled:

The family was not *Ithna'ashariyya* but *Nizari Ismailis*, who were not Muslims but Hindus by origin. As a result, Islamic inheritance laws did not apply.

With this judgment, SMS secured an extraordinary victory. Not only was he legally absolved of any obligation to share his wealth, but his control over both the assets of Aga Khan I and the community's ongoing religious tributes, was now formally recognized.

The Haji Bibi case had legitimized SMS as the undisputed owner of the *Nizari* Ismaili fortune. However, it also highlighted the fact that Nizaris were not Muslims.

A New Era of Opportunity

Whether SMS was divine is still debated, but at every turn, fortune seemed to smile upon him.

After all, he got away with declaring himself divine, successfully kept Muslim hardliners at bay given his un-Islamic lifestyle, avoided death penalty for treason in Britain, and out maneuvered income tax officials all his life.

But fate had one more boon in store for him.

Industrial Revolution

The eighteenth century ushered in the Industrial Revolution, transforming the way we live. Agriculture and primary industries gave way to mechanized manufacturing, leading to lower production costs, increased consumption, and, ultimately, increased personal wealth.

Initially, its benefits were concentrated in Western nations, but by the dawn of the twentieth century, the economic ripples had reached the developing world.

For the Nizari Ismailis—most of whom lived in India and East Africa—the financial impact was profound. Personal wealth and income rose to unprecedented heights, and with this newfound prosperity came an enhanced capacity to support religious causes.

SMS happened to be the Imam at this time of prosperity, and he was more than ready to rake in the windfall.

Moreover, as he was legally affirmed as the sole recipient of the community's tributes, he stood perfectly positioned to capitalize on this economic boom.

To his followers, this was a time of prosperity. To their Imam, it was divine providence, a God-sent opportunity for the God of the Nizari Ismailis.

As the personal incomes of millions of his followers surged, so did the *dasond* revenue flowing into SMS's coffers. Paid at 12.5% of an individual's income, tithe alone multiplied several times over, not to mention financial tributes under other headings.

In just a few years, SMS, the British pensioner had transformed into one of the richest men in the world!!

This material success was proudly displayed during SMS's jubilee celebrations, where his followers weighed him, first in gold, then in diamonds and eventually in platinum.

They sincerely believed that their prosperity was a direct result of his divine powers.

But for SMS, this was just the beginning. Based on what eventuated since, it is reasonable to infer that he embarked on a three-stage strategy to multiply the windfall many times over.

With greed at the center of his design, the strategy was inspired by commerce. The multi-level strategy was about milking the cash cow dry and most amazingly, to make them thank him for accepting their money!!

The Lure

Across religions—be it Hinduism, Islam, or Christianity—only a fraction of believers regularly attends places of worship. The Nizari Ismailis were no different until SMS worked his magic.

He reimagined the Jamaatkhana not merely as a place of worship, but as a spiritual enterprise—with himself as its sole beneficiary.

But how could he ensure higher attendance?
The genius transformed the Jamaatkhana into a

social and political hub, where worship came with entertainment!!

A place of worship where the faithful could celebrate their way to heaven!

The transformation started with a change in attire. Having adopted a Western look himself, SMS encouraged his followers to do the same. For women, this newfound freedom was revolutionary. They embraced fashion, dressing with glitter, elegance, and on occasion revealing a little skin. Naturally, this drew the men, who relished both the social scene and the opportunity to network for business.

After a brief, shirk-infested prayer session, the *Jamaatkhana* would erupt into a lively social gathering.

The lines between faith and festivity blurred as men and women enjoyed their new liberties all while earning a ticket to paradise.

The Elite Class

Alongside reshaping the social fabric of the *Jamaatkhana,* SMS moved to institutionalize the *Nizari* faith. He established a formal administrative structure, ensuring that the flow of wealth remained efficient and uninterrupted.

To achieve this, he handpicked the rich and

influential, appointing them to key leadership positions. These individuals would run the operations, acting as intermediaries between him and the community.

But loyalty demands incentive. In return for their services, SMS bestowed upon them grand honorific titles, a masterstroke in psychological persuasion.

He created a hierarchy of prestige, an illusion of power that secured an unwavering commitment to his cause of amassing wealth.

Those in his inner circle were anointed with titles such as *Vazir* (Prime Minister) and *Aitmadi* (Trustworthy), reinforcing their privileged status within the community.

An elite class was born!

Through this clever fusion of faith, wealth, and human psychology, SMS cemented his control, ensuring that the machinery of devotion remained well-oiled and profitable.

This was a win-win situation!

The elites gained prestige and social dominance, while SMS's coffers overflowed without lifting a finger.

The elites turned the *Jamaatkhana* into more than just a place of worship. It became a hub of influence in the marketplace where status was bought and displayed, connections were forged and food and entertainment took center stage. Marriage alliances were arranged, reputations were built, and yet, understanding faith, let alone Islam became an afterthought.

As the pull of social prestige and outlook grew stronger, dormant followers, those who had once remained on the fringes, found themselves gravitating toward the nearest *Jamatkhana.*

SMS had skillfully shepherded the flock into the club!

It was time to captivate!!

Mental Captivation

Modern research in psychiatry and social science sheds light on a paradox of human behavior. To understand irrational loyalty, particularly to cult leaders, we must first understand the mechanics of the human brain.

In her book *Brainwashing*, Kathleen Taylor, a research scientist at Oxford, refers to the brain as a *"Traitor in the Skull."* She explains how our neurophysiology leaves us vulnerable to manipulation.

The brain is composed of three main parts: the cerebrum, cerebellum, and brain stem. Within the cerebrum,

Cerebral cortex is divided into two hemispheres the right (RH) and the left (LH). The right hemisphere is associated with emotion, playing a key role in processing feelings and sensory perceptions. LH, on the other hand, is analytical and critical by nature and assesses information based on past records which we refer to as our experiences.

When we receive information, RH paints it with emotions, but it does not enter our belief system without LH's critical assessment. If the new information aligns with pre-existing beliefs, LH accepts it. If not, it is either rejected outright or scrutinized further.

Now, imagine someone indoctrinated from childhood to believe that the Aga Khan is divine. Their right hemisphere instantly infuses it with emotion, reverence, longing, and the dream of glimpsing him.

The information is then passed to LH for critical analysis. Since LH's stored memories reinforce the belief in his divinity, the claim is not questioned, and the information is accepted as truth.

He is accepted as God!

But what happens if someone suggests that SMS is a fraud? The left hemisphere (LH) of the brain will reject the idea because it contradicts stored records reinforced as beliefs.

Now, a child's brain is different physiologically as it is immature and lacks critical reasoning. The LH, which is responsible for logical and critical assessment, is underdeveloped.

Consequently, children often accept information without question, whether it is true or false. It is no wonder children are gullible and vulnerable to abuse!

For manipulators therefore, childhood is the perfect opportunity to instill ideas that will later be unquestioningly embraced.

A child will not argue, protest, or reject teaching, especially when they come from trusted figures like parents, teachers, or elders. Over time, repeated exposure to the same ideas forms an unshakable belief system that persists in adulthood.

During my visit to Mumbai in 2015, I decided to test this hypothesis on an Aga Khan devotee. Not just any devotee, but one of his most influential missionaries.

Babul Missionary was a revered figure within the Aga Khan community, recognized globally for his religious discourses.

One of my uncles, who had connections with him, arranged our meeting. However, he also warned the scholar that I had defected beyond redemption.

When we finally met in Bandra, a suburb of Mumbai, I immediately noticed something unusual. His charismatic demeanor was missing. The great scholar, known for his ever-present and contagious smile, appeared visibly tense.

I offered to buy him a coffee, but he politely declined. He wanted to end this encounter as quickly as possible. I, on the other hand, was determined to see if Taylor's theory held on the ground level.

On that day, standing in front of the scholar, memories of *Karimabad Jamaatkhana* came rushing back. Memories of my boyhood and then teenage years, when I had absorbed his teachings.

Back then, in a controlled environment, he had indoctrinated me with absolute authority without fear of challenge.

Today was different!!

He was outside that protective bubble of *Jamatkhana*. Today he was facing a rebel and anticipating him being taken to task.

It was no wonder he was tense!

The conversation that followed in *Hindi,* our local vernacular went something like this:

Me:

"I live in Australia and know of a family who are followers of Aga Khan. The family consists of a husband, a wife, and two young children. The husband has a mistress, something the wife is finding increasingly difficult to tolerate. My question is: Does this man's behavior align with the moral framework of being a Nizari Ismaili?"

Missionary:

"Look here, I am not qualified to answer such questions. You should ask your local Jamati leaders."

Me:

"I have never heard my Jamati leaders give discourses on morals and ethics, but you have. Please answer my question. How would you feel if the woman I'm talking about was your daughter?"

He now looked shaken, realizing exactly where this was going. His hesitation was brief but telling. Then, very reluctantly, he agreed.

Missionary:

"Okay... his behavior doesn't sound right. Is that all you want to know?"

Me:

"Yes, thank you."

A brief silence followed.

Sensing an opportunity, he turned to walk away. Just when he took his first step, I disturbed his flow.

Me:

"Just one more question, if you don't mind."

He froze mid-step…he was now visibly disturbed.

"You just agreed that the man's behavior was wrong. But what if I told you that Hazar Imam (Aga Khan) himself has engaged in similar behavior and even got caught?"

"Twice!!"

In the comfort of *Jamatkhana*, the respected missionary was renowned for quick responses to questions but today…he was struggling.

It was his turn to respond, and he didn't know how. I noticed a single bead of sweat trickled down his forehead, sliding down his face.

The silence stretched.

Finally, after what felt like an eternity, he gathered himself.

Missionary:

"It is an allegation meant to discredit Hazar Imam."

At that moment, I reached into my pocket and pulled out a newspaper clipping from The Telegraph, a UK publication, which details the specifics of Aga Khan's adultery case. (This can be googled)

Me:

"It is not an allegation. It is a conviction by the French courts. He was found guilty of adultery. Here is the proof."

That was the abrupt end of the conversation. The missionary froze for a moment then…took flight!!

Hurriedly, he crossed the narrow street and then, with one last glance over his shoulder, he turned toward me, his voice trembling with anger, he cursed me.

"Tum maroge!" (You will die)

Fate, however, had its own plans.

Almost a year after that encounter, Babul Missionary passed away. I sincerely hope he rests in eternal peace for he was a good man, only blinded by the system.

On a few occasions in my life, I have woken up at dawn to watch the darkness of the night run away from the rising sun. On that day, outside that *Jamatkhana*, I saw ignorance and blind faith personified by Babul missionary run from the light of truth contained in UK Telegraph article.

I walked away, satisfied that I had verified Taylor's theory to be credible.

Nazi lessons

It was evident that SMS had mastered the art of mental captivation, though how he became so proficient remains a mystery.

What is striking, however, is the uncanny resemblance between his methods and those of one of his infamous contemporaries: Adolf Hitler.

Hitler demonstrated with chilling precision how masses could be controlled through mind-captivation techniques, particularly repetition.

In 1918, after Germany's defeat in World War I, the Treaty of Versailles shattered the nation's spirit. The terms were brutal: Germany was forced to pay reparations in the billions while already on its knees, surrender vast territories, accept severe military restrictions, and cease arms production entirely.

The surviving German population struggled to come to terms with the humiliation. Among them was a young Adolf Hitler, then just a soldier seething with resentment. Blinded by his deep-seated hatred for Jews, whom he blamed for Germany's downfall, he began to fantasize about retribution.

As fate would have it, Hitler rose to power, his ascent fueled by brilliant oratory skills, a manipulative mind, a void where conscience should have been, and an unmatched understanding of human psychology.

He formed the Nazi Party, employing a calculated problem-solution approach. The Germans desperately longed to reclaim the lost glory of their nation. Hitler offered a solution, which was more of an illusion—one built on deception and blind faith. He convinced the masses that he alone was their savior, their Messiah, the man who would restore their golden past.

But how did he delude an entire nation?

Gustave Le Bon, a leading psychologist of his time, provided Hitler with the tools to manipulate the masses. Armed with psychological strategies, Hitler created the Ministry of Public Enlightenment and Propaganda, appointing Paul Joseph Goebbels as its head.

Nazi propaganda proved beyond doubt that once a population was indoctrinated and brainwashed, it could be coerced into giving of their loyalty, wealth, and even life.

Goebbels weaponized cinema, radio, and newspapers to craft a singular image: Hitler as a man of peace, the German Aryan race as superior, and their destiny as rulers of the world.

Tragically, this propaganda machine fueled the persecution of Jews scapegoated as the root of Germany's problems. What began as vilification soon escalated to systematic extermination.

In *Mein Kampf,* Hitler revealed one of his most powerful psychological weapons: repetition. He understood that the human mind, when exposed to the same message repeatedly, would eventually accept it as truth regardless of its accuracy.

After all, the law of propaganda dictates that a falsehood repeated a thousand times is far easier to believe than an unfamiliar truth heard just once.

Years later, Tom Stafford, a professor of psychology and cognitive science at the University of Sheffield, explored this very concept in his book, *For Argument's Sake: Evidence that Reason Can Change Minds.* Stafford described the illusion of truth as a cognitive bias where repetition alone increases a statement's perceived validity.

He cited a study conducted at Vanderbilt University, published in the Journal of Experimental Psychology. The study involved eighty participants who were asked to evaluate the truthfulness of various statements.

In one experiment, forty participants rated each statement's accuracy on a six-point scale. In another, a separate group of forty simply labeled each statement as true or false.

In both cases, repetition significantly increased the likelihood of a statement being perceived as true even when it contradicted well-known facts. For instance, when participants repeatedly heard the claim, "Oslo is the capital of Finland," many came to accept it despite knowing that Helsinki is Finland's actual capital.

SMS took inspiration from Hitler's problem-solution approach and the use of psychology to manipulate his following. However, unlike the German problem, he focused on the ever-present primordial problem of eternal suffering in hell.

He magnified this fundamental human dread, embedding it deep into the minds of his followers. Then, he offered the only escape convincing them that he was God incarnate, who had come to redeem them.

To get the ball rolling, he convinced his followers that they were sinners and destined for eternal suffering!!

To achieve this goal, he established the Recreation Club (RC), his version of Nazi Ministry of Public Enlightenment and Propaganda.

"So that you can work for the world during the daytime, and for the religion at night hour."

SMS funded RC generously, ensuring its growth and influence. He equipped it with a printing press that published the weekly Ismaili magazine, a tool that reinforced his teachings and ideological messaging.

Before long, RC evolved into more than just a gathering space, it became an institution, training missionaries and religious education teachers to spread his doctrine. By 1940, RC was renamed: the Ismailia Association (IA)

Its mission was divided into three key functions: training *waezeens* (missionaries) in the art of propaganda, indoctrinating children in Religious Education Centers (REC), where they would be immersed in IA's twisted narrative; and lastly, establishing a spiritual leadership hierarchy that would oversee the continuous cycle of revenue-generating rituals and ceremonies participated in by devotees… from cradle to grave.

Children as young as five were exposed to IA's sinister content, a deadly cocktail of fantastical *ginanic* material, distorted Islamic principles, Hindu mythology, and fabricated Ismaili history.

This meticulously crafted blend of ideas ensured that, from a young age, followers absorbed a belief system so deeply embedded in their minds that it became nearly impossible to question or break free from."

To solidify his control, it was paramount that SMS's system instilled a deep sense of guilt within his followers. Every breath they took, every moment they lived, had to be a reminder of their sinfulness and their inevitable drift toward the horrors of hell.

It was crucial to his strategy that his followers believed with strong conviction that they were sinners.... from top to toe!!

Towards this end, IA designed ingenious and multiple methods to make them confess to sins they had not committed.... while filling SMS's coffers!!

The Sinner

When a child is born into a Nizari family, the newborn, pure, innocent, and defenseless is brought to the *Jamatkhana* for the *bayah* (oath of allegiance) ceremony. It involves the newborn swearing allegiance to the Imam via his parents.

This ceremony, according to the *ginans,* is a recognition of Imam as the child's spiritual parent, granting him dominion over their body, mind, and most significantly his wealth.

The ceremony also marks the child's first official declaration that he is a sinner from top to toe. From that moment forward, the child may or may not sin through life, he would constantly reaffirm his sinfulness, confess time and time again, that he is a sinner from top to toe seeking absolution.

With time confessing to sins he has not committed becomes a mechanical action.

As previously discussed, repetition was one of Adolf Hitler's deadliest tools for control. SMS would wield it with equal, if not a greater force.

IA's mind-altering designs compelled followers psychologically to repeatedly confess their sins. Through daily *Jamatkhana* sessions and numerous *majlises* (religious meetings), devotees would be immersed in a constant cycle of rituals, prayers, *ginans,* sermons, supplications, and *farmans.* All reinforcing a singular and unshakable belief:

I am a sinner!!

Many religions offer acts of atonement. In Islam, a Muslim performs *Istighfar* as part of their worship of Allah, seeking forgiveness for their wrongdoings.

However, SMS's agenda was total submission of his followers. It required systematic and constant reminders of sin and the need for redemption.

Besides, SMS couldn't afford to leave the matter of deeds and sins solely between his followers and God. If the Almighty up in the sky were to forgive their sins, how would he collect spiritual revenue?

Therefore, he encouraged his followers to come to the *Jamatkhana* regularly. Once there they would participate in the rituals, not only to continually affirm their identity as sinners from top to toe but to pay for the absolution of their sins!!

This constant repetition of their inherent sinfulness would reinforce their dependence on him for salvation, ensuring they remained tethered to his influence, paying penance both literally and figuratively.

Dua Karawi (confession of sins)

Istighfar was incompatible with SMS's designs. After all, its practice was rooted in genuine repentance for his purposes. To circumvent this, SMS a designed a unique ritual inspired, not by Islam but… the Christian practice of confession.

In Christianity, the act of confession involves a believer confessing their sins to a priest, offering a sincere admission of their wrongdoings. They then pray for an act of contrition, expressing remorse and a resolve not to sin again. This ritual serves as both spiritual cleansing and a reaffirmation of faith.

SMS adapted this concept and tweaked it to suit his purpose.

His ritual involved the sinner facing the *Mukhi* (the priest) who is seated on the floor, offer him money, lock eyes with him, fold his hands in submission, and make a verbal declaration:

Tobo taksir daar, bando sir ta pa gunegar, ya shah tu gunah bakshe bakshanhaar.

Meaning:

"I repent, I repent, I am a sinner from head to toe. O my lord (the Imam), please forgive my sins, only You can."

The *Mukhi* accepts the money and, in turn, prays for the sinner. The sinner then takes his seat in the congregation, feeling reassured that his sins are forgiven.

Soon a *ginan* is recited, reminding him that all sins are his own, and it is only the Imam, the Merciful, who could forgive.

Ejee bhalee bataavo, ya shaah buree tajaavo, har doe haath tamaare, ya shaah tere taraf ko karam hameshaa, paap dosh hamaaraa.

"O Hazar Imam! Help me to do the good and avoid evil. Both are entirely in Your power, O Lord! Mercy comes always from You, and the sins and errors are from me."

This is followed by congregational supplications, known as *tasbih*, where the sinner once again seeks forgiveness for their sins.

"Ya Ali, ya Hazar Imam, tu asaja kul gunah maaf kar."

(O my lord, the Imam, forgive all my sins.)

These methods would be employed twice daily during Jamatkhana sessions. Beyond these, the sinner would be given further opportunities.

During various majlises (religious meetings), not only would they repeat the above rituals but participate in further resembling ones.

Chhanta (holy water sprinkling)

Gunah bakshamni or the forgiveness of sins chhanta.

In essence, this ritual is a repetition of *Dua karawi*, or confession of sins ritual. This time, however, the sinner faces the *Mukhi* while kneeling (instead of standing), offering him money, locking eyes, folding their hands in submission, and making a similar declaration:

"Bando gunegaar, gat bakshe shah pir bakshe."

I am a sinner; may the commune and Imam forgive me.

The *Mukhi* responds:

"Hazar Imam bakshe."

May the Imam forgive

The sinner repeats this confession three times, and with each repetition, the *Mukhi* offers a prayer in return.

After the third confession, the *Mukhi* dips his fingers in the holy water (touched by Imam), sprinkles it over the followers' faces, and offers further prayers.

This ritual is known as *gunah bakshamni* or the forgiveness of sins *chhanta.*

Ruhani Roshni (spiritual light) Chhanta

A key distinction between religions and cults lies in their concept of God: In most religions, God is considered distant, residing in the sky or remaining inaccessible. In contrast, in cults, God takes human form and is accessible to his devotees.

Accordingly, in Agakhanism, the Imam is the divine in human form, and hence it is no wonder that his followers go to great lengths to achieve his *deedar,* the physical sighting.

However, meeting the Imam physically is only possible when he visits their *Jamatkhana…* an event that may not occur for them.

To counter this problem, SMS devised an ingenious scheme whereby, not only would his followers be blessed with his *deedar* (without giving the *deedar*) and fill his coffers at the same!!

The seekers desperate for his physical *deedar* were encouraged to seek his *Noorani Deedar* (Spiritual Sighting) instead. Physically, he may or may not meet every spiritual child but in spirit he is ever present to be seen by one and all, the celestial being suggested!!

In Nizari terminology, this idea of being blessed by Imam's spiritual form, is referred to as seeing the *Noor of the Imam.* It is believed that one who witnesses the *Noor* (light) of the Imam becomes sinless. Therefore, during every *Jamatkhana* session, they pray:

"Ya Ali Ya Hazar Tu Asa ke tojo Zaheri ane Noorani deedar Naseeb kar

O our Lord, Our Hazar Imam, please bless us with your physical and spiritual deedar.

But the question endures: Where does one go to see the *Noor, the spiritual deedar*?

The answer lies in the membership of a *majalis* known as *Bait ul Khayal (house of thoughts or wisdom)*

At this juncture it is important to note that there are thirteen *majalises* on offer and each one features its revenue generating rituals and ceremonies.

In any case, those followers who wish to see Imam's *Noor* would need to join this *majalis*. To be included, one needs to pay an entry fee, attend a daily session at 3.45 am, and meditate for an hour.

The ever-resourceful system commissioned an additional revenue generating *Chhanta* which would remove all sins and thus allow the *Noor* to become manifest.

It is referred to as, *Ruhani Roshni" or Spiritual Light Chhanta.*

Mahadan (Day of Judgement) Chhanta

In one of his *farmans,* SMS expressed a desire that none of his followers should leave this world a sinner. Being a man of his word, he ensured that every follower participated in a *Mahadan (Day of Judgement) Chhanta* to cleanse their sins before departing the world.

Yes, it was yet another revenue generating ritual but where did SMS get the inspiration for *Mahadan?*

The answer lies in the human emotion of fear!!

The greatest motivator of humankind, fear displaces reason and logic, even in those who are otherwise sensible.

History is a witness that to control us, people have been made to fear each other, fear people of other beliefs, fear other countries and ultimately…hell.

SMS had inherited *ginanic* literature, a wealth of material to reinforce fear in his followers' hearts. According to this literature, in hell, sinners would be struck with iron instruments breaking their limbs and when they are struck over their heads, their brains would protrude out from their ears!!

One such ginan is *Dil na daga bande*

Ejee ja(n)tr zaalee jeevddo saannseeye toddaavshe, taare jeevddo karashe pukaar jeere.

Meaning:

Iron instruments will sever the body's limbs, bound by the chains of sinful actions. In that moment of agony, the soul will lament its fate.

Yet another ginan *'Door desh thi'* also provides a graphic example of human torture.

Ejee bhulo te maathaano bhejo kaane neesarashejee,
teel teelnaa lekhaa saaheb leshejee

Meaning

If you have forgotten the gravity of your sin, then the
Lord will punish you in a way so severe that your brain will
almost burst from your ears. The Lord will account for every
action.

In daily *Jamatkhana* sessions, the sinner would be reminded repeatedly via *ginans,* sermons and *farmans* that they face suffering in hell, in case they were thinking of not conforming.

It is no wonder, the petrified sinner spends their entire lives paying, praying, and participating in countless rituals, hoping for forgiveness and mercy.

Then death knocks at the door!!

The sinner is still not sure if he would die sinless. He is still not sure if he is destined to endure endless suffering in hell.

To resolve their anxiety, SMS was on standby!!

He suggested that departing souls be given a *Mahadan Chhanta.* After all, it is a final cleanse, which would render them sinless, allowing a smooth transition from this world to the bliss of heaven!!

The question endures: do they really die sinless? How was one to know? After all, no one has come back to tell the story.

True, no one knows…except followers of Agakhan!!

They know, without a doubt, that the deceased is in hell! Why else would they continue to pay and pray perpetually for the liberation of the departed soul?

Once the body is laid to rest, the funeral party embarks on a pilgrimage back to *Jamatkhana*, called *ziyarat*. Here, they once again pay and pray for the forgiveness of the deceased's sins!!

But these rituals don't end here!

Special *majlises* are arranged, involving the entire congregation, to pay and pray for forgiveness of the deceased's sins!!

In fact, these sessions will become a ritual themselves!!

This means each deceased, after having paid and prayed to SMS throughout his life, will continue to pay from the depths of his grave…. into eternity!

The moral of the story, Agakhan follower will always remain a sinner… dead or alive!!

Raiding the back pocket

Now that SMS had lured most followers into the newly found social club and had mentally captivated them with fear, it was time to raid the back pocket.

In relation to money and faith, the Holy Quran says:

Alms are meant for the poor, the needy, and those tasked with administering the funds; for those whose hearts have been reconciled to the truth; for those in bondage or in debt; in the cause of Allah; and for travelers in need. This is what Allah has ordained, for He is all-knowing and wise. (Sura Al Tawbah)

Zakat, one of the five pillars of Islam, means *'that which purifies.'* While the Holy Quran does not specify the exact calculation method, it is customary to pay 2.5% of one's wealth.

However, the scripture clearly outlines the beneficiaries: the poor, the indebted, those who work for Islam, new converts, travelers, slaves, those whose hearts are to be reconciled, and *zakat* collectors.

Therefore, according to Islamic doctrine, the primary purpose of *zakat* is to aid those in need.

The *Nizari Ismailis* disagreed!!

To them the religious revenue personally belonged to the Imam. In fact, this was highlighted by the Haji Bibi Case of 1908. The judge had ruled that the followers of SMS were essentially Hindus, and thus Islamic law did not apply to them. Consequently, SMS was not obligated to share his wealth or income with anyone which included the poor and the needy.

Dasond, unlike *Zakat,* must be paid by rich and poor alike. Notably, no one would hover over your shoulder to collect it. Instead, the Nizari Ismaili followers pay out of a deeply ingrained fear and relentless psychological coercion culminating in an unwavering belief system.

In medieval times, the Nizari Ismaili propagation campaigns were funded by *dasond*, the 10% religious tax.

With time, however, these campaigns faded into obscurity and so did the need for such funding.

But SMS not only revived it but added an extra 2.5%, for his role as a "Pir"!! It is noteworthy that the Ismaili doctrine identifies the Imam as a divine guide, whilst the Pir's role is to make the person of the Imam known.

At any rate, to enforce the inflated tax, SMS relied on IA, the propaganda machine. *Waezes, ginans,* and *farmans* were mobilized, especially when large crowds were expected.

One *waez* (delivered post SMS era) had a lasting impact on me. It suggested that those who didn't offer *dasond* were worse than... a monkey.

The Monkey Waez

Ramayana, the Hindu mythological epic, tells of *Lord Rama's* favorite fruit, the bullock's heart, which the Hindus named *Ramphal* after him. His wife, *Sita,* preferred the apple custard, which was renamed *Sitaphal.*

During his *waez,* a Nizari scholar, late Bahadurali Rajani, remarked, *"Give any monkey a Sitaphal, and he will devour it; but try giving him a Ramphal, and he will never touch it, no matter how hungry he is."*

Why?

Because it is the monkeys due to his Lord, his *dasond,* a sacred offering that the monkey will never touch!

(The reader may google *Bahadur Rajani's* waezes on *dasond)*

In addition, there are countless *ginans* available to remind the devotee, relentlessly, of the importance of *dasond.*

Ejee dharam no bhed dasho(n)d-j kaheeye, dasho(n)d veenaa paar na laiye.

Only through dasond are the inner mysteries of religion revealed. Without it, one cannot attain salvation.

And, of course, there was SMS himself, playing his part.

"You will be able to do Ibadat (devotion) forever and derive its benefits as long as the world and the earth exist. But Dasond will not last forever. What of the miserable souls who did not pay Dasond in the past? That is why those of you endowed with wealth must urgently undertake this work; otherwise, you will regret it greatly."

Payday

SMS had revolutionized Nizari Ismailism, in more than one way!! However, establishing a *majalis* for collection of *dasond* was a masterstroke!!

The Islamic (Hijri) calendar follows a lunar cycle. Therefore, *Chaandraat,* the night of the new moon, holds particular significance in Islam. Accordingly, SMS established and named the new *majlis, Chaandraat* which would be held every new moon night, as it does to this day.

Not only did *Chandraat* systemize and regularize collection of holy revenue but established yet another channel to milk the cash cow!!

After all, the new *majalis* would feature rituals and ceremonies attracting further revenue apart from the submission of *dasond*!!

Jubilees

Eight of SMS's alleged ancestors had ruled as Caliphs during the golden period of the *Fatimid Caliphate* in the Middle Ages.

Accordingly, SMS had long harbored a burning desire to follow in their footsteps. As discussed earlier, he had even begged the British for a piece of land to rule over, but his request was rejected. Though the dream seemed to crumble, his yearning to be treated like a monarch turned into an obsession.

In 1936, he took matters into his own hands to fulfill this fantasy!

Historically, Jubilees marked a milestone in a monarch's reign, and SMS decided to celebrate the golden jubilee of his Imamate.

On 18 January 1936, 30,000 of his Indian followers, along with a few dignitaries, gathered at Hasanabad in Bombay. The neighborhoods of South Bombay where the *Khojas* lived were illuminated in preparation. The event was lavish, pompous, and noisy. Rich and poor alike had traveled from far and wide to see their Imam adorned as a king…that he wasn't!!

The air buzzed with anticipation as his arrival grew nearer. At 11 a.m., his entourage arrived, escorted by the Bombay Police. Thousands of eager followers, desperate for a glimpse, nearly caused a stampede.

Once everyone was settled, SMS inspected the guard of honor prepared by the *Khojas*. He was dressed in a purple *sherwani* and a green turban, elegantly accompanied by his French wife, Andree, in a light green *saree*. His mother, *Lady Aly Shah*, was already seated on a dais.

SMS's speech was met with cheers, followed by the much-anticipated weighing ceremony. He struggled to fit his 230-pound frame onto one side of the scale while gold ingots worth Rs 3,30,000 were placed on the other.

The jubilee funds raised by the community as a gift for SMS, were later 'donated' by SMS for community welfare.

Then the *Khoja* leaders thanked him for 'his' generosity!!

SMS may have been mocked for his monarch pretension, jubilees only served to further enrich his already overflowing coffers.

A similar celebration at the Aga Khan Club in Nairobi saw 12,000 Khojas and a few local dignitaries in attendance.

A decade later, on 10 March 1946, SMS's Diamond Jubilee celebrations took place at Brabourne Stadium in Bombay. The stadium was packed with 70,000 followers and a select group of dignitaries. SMS arrived at cheers of *Khojas*, dressed in a tunic and turban.

But all eyes were on Yvette, his latest wife!

The Goddess was draped in a white sari studded with diamonds, estimated to be worth $1,80,000.

SMS soon reclaimed attention when he stood to deliver a short speech, greeted by chants of '*Aga Khan Zindabad*' '*long live Aga Khan.*'

Then came the weighing ceremony. Rumors had circulated that SMS had gained weight in anticipation. It was now time to confirm. The scale tipped at a staggering 243.5 pounds.

The ceremony raised Rs 750,000, funded by the followers…some filthy rich, others hopelessly poor.

Once again, SMS proudly declared that the funds would be used for community welfare. The Diamond Jubilee Trust was formed as a result, to help small business owners.

However, its objective would not be charity, rather profiting from providing interest-bearing loans.

The gullible followers' Jubilee gift had returned to them as a… debt!!

The second leg of the celebration took place in Dar es Salaam, Tanzania, on 9 August 1946. Yet, what should have been a joyous occasion was overshadowed by SMS contracting pneumonia.

After returning to Europe, he was diagnosed with prostate cancer. Despite facing significant health challenges, SMS proved resilient, surviving long enough to witness his Platinum Jubilee—though in noticeably frail health.

The celebration, delayed multiple times, finally occurred in 1954 at Hotel Semiramis in Cairo, attended by a small gathering of a few hundred loyal followers.

The grandeur and fervor of previous jubilees were notably absent, as was Aly, his elder son.

SMS received a £300,000 cheque as a token of appreciation. Later that year, he was presented with another cheque for £260,000 in Karachi.

From that point onward, however, his health declined rapidly.

Death and Succession

Although SMS had led a long and full life, his health was never robust. Particularly, after World War II, he endured a range of ailments: cancer, heart disease, diabetes, lumbago, sciatica, cirrhosis of the liver, insomnia, depression, and impotence.

It was time to appoint a successor!

Given the 1,300-year-old tradition, Aly, his eldest son, seemed the natural choice. Accordingly, back in 1930, SMS had sent nineteen-year-old Aly to Syria with a message for his followers:

"I am sending my beloved son (Aly) to you; you should consider him as equivalent to my own presence. I am sending the prince in the capacity of my heir apparent."

Then, in 1951, during an interview, SMS reconfirmed Aly as his successor. Based on this confirmation, Aly publicly affirmed his nomination in a press interview.

However, neither the all-knowing father nor the son was aware at that time that Aly would not be the next Nizari Imam nor the Aga Khan!!

Both were oblivious of a crucial discussion regarding his succession at the India Office in London. A note in its archives dated 1955 expresses British concerns about Aly. The author of the note was Sir Gilbert Laithwaite, who had written to Douglas Dodds Parker, the parliamentary undersecretary, as follows:

"Mr. Mott Radclyffe, M.P., has had a fly dropped over him regarding the 'succession' by Aly Khan: Will His Majesty recognize him as Aga when the current Aga Khan dies, given his history of wild behavior?"

Aly's promiscuity, failed marriages, and gambling addiction had long been a source of embarrassment not just to SMS, but also to his followers.

SMS knew Aly was his reflection, albeit one who lacked his far-sightedness, as well as his sharp, calculating, and manipulative mind.

Coincidentally, the same year in which Laithwaite's memo was written, SMS amended his will and deposited it in Lloyd's Bank, Paris. The new version was kept secret, even from close family, especially from Aly.

A couple of years later the angel of death knocked at God's door!!

On 11 July 1957, the SMS's family and leadership had gathered at Villa Barakat in Versoix, Switzerland. At precisely 00:40 am, Miss Whitaker, his secretary, solemnly announced,

"His Highness has died."

The legend's heart had failed.

The following day the will, dated 25 May 1955, was read.

Addressing his succession, it read:

"In light of the profound shifts in the world in recent years, including the advent of atomic science, I am convinced it is in the best interests of the Shia Muslim Ismaili community that I be succeeded by a young man raised and nurtured in this new era—a man who will bring a fresh perspective to the office of Imam. For this reason, although he is not currently one of my heirs, I appoint my grandson, Karim, son of my son, Aly Salomone Khan, to succeed me as Aga Khan, Imam and Pir of all my Shia Ismaili followers."

The will further stated:

"My successor shall, during the first seven years of his Imamate, be guided on questions of general Imamate policy by my third wife (actually fourth), Yvette, known as Yve Blanche Labruse, the Begum Aga Khan. She has been

familiar for many years with the problems facing my followers, and in her judgment, I place the greatest confidence."

Aly was devastated.

Not only had the dream of becoming the next Aga Khan been shattered, but he also found himself in a bizarre situation:

He was now a spiritual son to his own son!!

However, solace came in the arms of his latest girlfriend, Bettina, who wrote:

"To Aly, it seemed that his father's preference for his son was a form of public humiliation. He was never quite the same after that day. His deep sadness hid behind a life of increasingly detached and inhuman activity."

Aly may have been devastated by his father's will, but it was the same will that exposed Agakhanism, in at least two significant ways:

First, the myth of the Imam as *Aql al-Kul*, the all-knowing, exploded in the face of his followers. SMS had no idea that Aly would not be the next Aga Khan, despite having nominated him in 1930 and 1951.

Second, *Mata Salamat* Yvette Blanche Labrousse became the new Imam's guide for seven years, contradicting Shia Nizari doctrine, which dictates that the Imam is the divine guide for all of humanity.

Furthermore, the will revealed that SMS was not married before having two children with Theresa Magliano. Instead, he had made a verbal *Muta'h* contract, a form of legal prostitution, in exchange for a 10,000 francs dowry.

During his long and eventful life, SMS, HH Sultan Mahomed Shah, known as Aga Khan III, left a lasting impact on people and events across the globe.

Yet, his greatest legacy lies in shaping Nizari Ismailism into Agakhanism, a resilient religio-commercial system—one that endures into the twenty-first century.

Chapter 4

Adventures of Prince Alykhan

In the prologue of *Aly: A Biography,* author Leonard Slater wrote:

"Moving out along East River Drive, we passed a red convertible, its top unreasonably down, a pretty redhead at the wheel, alone."

Aly signaled for the chauffeur to slow down. He peered out, waved until he caught the young woman's eye, then swung entirely around for a final look through the rear window.

"If only I had more time," he muttered, shifting his attention back to Ross.

Aly Salomone Khan, accompanied by Leonard Slater and his adviser Jack Ross, was enroute to New York's Idlewild Airport when this moment occurred.

Born on July 13, 1911, in Turin, Italy, to SMS and Theresa Magliano, Aly was a man who truly knew how to savor every moment of life.

Prince Aly Khan

A truly inspirational figure, he bred and raced horses that triumphed in prestigious events like the Derby. He flew a single-engine plane from Bombay to Singapore without a radio, he was an avid big-game hunter and his passion for speed was evident in his love for racing cars, a passion that would unfortunately lead to his untimely death.

Aly enjoyed champagne, a bet at the casino, and represented Pakistan at the United Nations, where he went on to become the vice president of the General Assembly.

However, what truly brought him international fame was his ability to seduce women!

A true Casanova, debonair, handsome, and dashing Aly had an almost supernatural charm that rendered women powerless to resist him. While his father relied on the *"I am rich"* trick to woo women, Aly played the '*I will die without you*' card with deadly precision.

As if his charm wasn't enough, he was also rumored to be a love machine. Legends swirled around his technique of dipping his hand in icy water to 'prolong' the session, or employing an ancient Arabic technique called *Imsak,* which involved focusing the mind to increase stamina.

Whether these tales were true remains uncertain, but what is clear is that he lived a life rich with passion and intrigue.

A Victim of Child Neglect

In his adolescence, Aly became an orphan, left vulnerable by both his father's neglect and his mother's untimely death. The psychological impact of their absence was profound and lasting.

"Physical abuse is only one form of child abuse. Neglect and emotional abuse can be just as damaging.

However, because they are more subtle, others are less likely to intervene. One example of emotional neglect is limited physical contact with the child, especially in early childhood."

Dr. Anthony Komaroff, professor at Harvard University

Dr. Martin Teicher, a neuroscientist and associate professor of psychiatry at Harvard, has found in his research that childhood neglect can result in abnormal brainwave patterns, one potential consequence being sexual promiscuity.

Aly was a living example of Dr Teicher's work.

Margaret

As a teenager, Aly's first serious romance was with Margaret Whigham, a strikingly beautiful young woman and the daughter of a business tycoon, George Whigham. Though they were eager to marry, George disapproved of the relationship. Aly perceived the rejection to be racially motivated, especially after George had publicly called him a *"nigger."*

Joan

Then, an Englishwoman named Joan Guiness entered his life. Though married to Thomas Loel Guiness, a merchant banker, and mother to their son, Patrick, she was about to encounter an unexpected twist in her life.

Joan Guiness (Tajudawla)

In the summer of 1933, when Thomas was away on a work assignment, Joan attended a dinner party. Seated on her table among six guests, Aly was a stranger. However, throughout the evening, Aly's gaze remained fixed on her.

Then what Aly did, only he could do!!

He leaned across the table and said to Joan:

"Darling, will you marry me?"

Everyone froze but Joan understandably was in a state of shock!

After a few moments, Joan managed to regain her composure. With a voice that trembled slightly, she explained that she was happily married and had a son.

Little did she know that she was dealing with Aly, the renowned Casanova.

Leaving the hall, although shaken, she was thankful the episode was over. However, she was unaware that another surprise was awaiting her at the hotel suite.

Every inch of the room was filled with bouquets, one of which carried a message that read,

"I will die without you."

Joan, young and beautiful, found herself tempted. She had longed for intimacy due to her husband's frequent business trips. Then a dashing prince appeared, out of a fairy tale, and proposed a relationship.

She succumbed to his irresistible charm!

However, what began as an affair was soon discovered by Thomas, who wasted no time filing for divorce. The High Court of Justice in London dissolved the marriage, citing evidence that Joan had engaged in multiple acts of adultery with Prince Aly S. Khan between 17 and 20 April 1935 at the Ritz Hotel.

The court awarded custody of their son, Patrick, to Thomas.

Aly married Joan on 18 May 1936. Seven months later, she gave birth to a son… Karim who would go on to become Aga Khan IV. While the birth itself was not premature, it was conceived outside of wedlock, making it, by legal standards, illegitimate. From an Islamic perspective, the birth had complex and serious implications.

Marriage with a *kafir* (non-Muslim) is considered invalid and hence the newborn is not only illegitimate but a result of *Zina* (adultery), a serious crime punishable by death in Islam.

In any case, Joan would later give Aly another son, Amyn Mohammad.

With time, Joan realized that Aly was not cut out for family life. His numerous extramarital affairs were something Joan tried and often failed to ignore. Yet nothing could have prepared her for the arrival of… a Hollywood megastar.

Rita

Elsa Maxwell, an American socialite, author, and prominent Hollywood figure, once remarked:

"When Aly fell in love with a woman, it was always with passion, madly and deeply. The only catch was, it might last no longer than a single night."

One evening, she hosted an exclusive party at the Summer Casino in Cannes. Among the select guests was Rita Hayworth, the epitome of Hollywood glamour, and Aly, the Casanova.

The chemistry between Aly and Rita was immediate... fire met fire; beauty met charm... igniting a fierce explosion of passion.

At the time, Rita had recently separated from her estranged husband, Orson Welles, the renowned Hollywood actor, director, and producer. She had a young daughter, Rebecca, from the marriage. As for Aly, he was married with two sons, Karim and Amyn.

For Joan, the Rita-Aly affair was the final straw.

She divorced Aly!

Meanwhile, Aly moved in with Rita. The proposal came soon after, but to Aly's surprise, Rita declined. Her secretary, Shifra Haran, suggested that although Rita was charmed by Aly, she felt his social and cultural background was incompatible with hers. Besides, Aly's reputation as a playboy didn't help.

Rita had heard stories such as Aly would bid farewell to one woman and have another waiting for him.

Soon, Rita traveled to Hollywood to fulfill her commitments with Columbia Pictures. Aly followed her to the U.S. and rented a house across the street from hers. Flowers, gifts, and letters began arriving, each one implying that he could not live without her.

Eventually, Rita gave in!

The couple returned to Paris, with little Rebecca in tow. They soon headed to Gstaad to celebrate the new year, fully aware that Joan and her boys were living there.

The couple's choice of Gstaad made headlines.

The People magazine suggested:

"This affair is an insult to all decent women."

Rita caused quite a stir in Gstaad, particularly at Le Rosey, the school where Aly's children attended. After her visit, Karim and his younger brother, Amyn, were given a new identity as the stepsons of film star Rita Hayworth.

Apart from dealing with the media's condemnation of their relationship, Aly had one more obstacle to face.... his father.

SMS despised Aly's relationship with Rita. However, he relented once he was told that Rita was already pregnant with Aly's child.

Doomed Marriage

The wedding date was set for May 27, 1949!

As the date drew nearer, Rita grew increasingly nervous. After all, she was about to marry the most promiscuous man in Europe.

Her ex-husband, Wells, happened to be in Rome at the time. Rita sent him a telegram asking for an urgent meeting. Wells, sensitive to her concerns, advised her to go through with the marriage. If it didn't work out, she could always seek a divorce.

Aly and Rita's wedding quickly became the most talked-about media event of the year. After a civil ceremony at the Cannes Town Hall, a Muslim ritual followed, blending Islamic tradition with glamour.

Aly and Rita wedding

Once the ceremony concluded, the newlyweds met SMS's followers. In keeping with Hindu custom, *Khojas* touched Rita's feet and offered her gifts, for she had become their Goddess.

The celebration culminated in an extravagant reception at Aly's Château l'horizon, where 500 guests were treated to an unforgettable evening with family pool filled with champagne!!

During the event, Rita's business manager, Lee Ellroy, recounted an unusual moment. Aly had invited him to the Cannes casino for a night out. As they enjoyed drinks, Aly casually asked, *"You've been here a week, haven't you?"* After Lee nodded, Aly vanished briefly, returning with two attractive women, one of whom was a breezy blonde.

"Take your pick," Aly offered.

When Lee declined, Aly simply shrugged and disappeared with the blonde.

As is often the case, relationships falter when they are formed out of infatuation and lust rather than love. For Aly, the initial fire of passion began to dim, and Rita openly admitted she was fed up with life with him.

"I love Aly very much. He's kind, but he doesn't understand what it takes to build a family," she would later confess. "He's obsessed with gambling, horse racing, and big-game hunting. He's a playboy, and I'm the one holding things together, working year-round in Hollywood. Aly's reckless spending leaves me to support us both.

Seven months later, on December 28, 1949, Rita gave birth to Aly's daughter, Yasmin. Meanwhile, SMS found Aly's carefree attitude increasingly troubling. As a public figure, and God to millions, his successor's behavior shattered the illusion of divinity his followers once held.

But how could he convince Aly to change?

One way, he thought, was to get Aly to spend more time with his followers. Not only would it keep him out of trouble, but it would also help him adjust to his future role as Imam. He ordered Aly and Rita to visit East Africa.

Once Rita's two girls were settled with a nanny at l'horizon, the couple left for Zanzibar.

However, the visit proved far from pleasant. The couple quarreled—sometimes violently. Aly would attend the *Jamatkhanas* to meet his father's followers, while Rita struggled to pass the time. One day, without informing Aly, she chartered a plane to France, retrieved the girls from l'horizon, and flew to New York.

Once there, she did two things: first, she initiated a divorce, citing *"extreme cruelty, entirely mental in nature"* as the reason; second, she demanded $3 million for Yasmin's trust account.

By January 26, 1953, she had secured the divorce and gained custody of Yasmin. As far as Aly was concerned, he was never short of love!

Once again, he fell in "love" and once again with a Hollywood film star…Gene Tierney.

SMS was furious and gave Aly an ultimatum!

Gene or the Imamate?

Aly chose Imamate!!

Later, he regretted his decision, not only because SMS dumped him anyway but because it sent Gene to a mental institution.

During the affair with Aly, she was struggling with a mental illness following the birth of a physically retarded child.

Aly's rejection triggered a mental collapse, and she had to be admitted to a mental institution where she was treated for nearly two years.

Aly with Gene

The media frenzy surrounding Aly's relationships intensified. With the Gene affair however, SMS found himself caught up in the circus.

He was far from happy!!

His greatest dilemma was how his followers would ever accept Aly as their Imam given his tarnished reputation. After all, SMS had been entrusted with preserving a 1,300-year-old tradition of father-to-son succession.

Though SMS had another son, Sadri (Sadruddin, Aly's stepbrother), he was not an option. The nomination for Sadri would further highlight Aly's flaws.

Ultimately, SMS made a bold and unprecedented decision… breaking the Shia Ismaili tradition.

He bypassed both his sons and nominated his grandson Karim, as his successor as discussed!!

Final Moments

Aly was involved in countless affairs: Margaret Whigham, Joan Guiness, Rita Hayworth, Gene Tierney, Joan Fontaine, Nancy Masseroni, Lise Bourdin, Liana Zafferani, Irene Papas, Irene Leher, Yvonne De Carlo—and the list goes on.

In her autobiography, *No Bed of Roses*, Joan Fontaine described the thorns in her life.

Aly Khan was a fairy-tale prince, and he knew it. Like a butterfly, he flitted from flower to flower, never staying long.

Zsa Zsa Gabor also spoke of him.

The secret to Aly's success lay in his singular focus. He knew how to make a woman feel as though he would perish without her. He pursued me for years, the sweet thing. I would tell him, 'No, no,' but he never gave up.

After Gene, Aly embarked on yet another relationship. This time with an Italian model, Bettina Graziani.

Finally, she would become his last girlfriend…tragically outside of his choice.

On May 12, 1960, his pattern of reckless and uncontrolled promiscuous behavior ended abruptly. While enroute to a party with Bettina, his Lancia sports car collided head-on with another vehicle.

Aly with Bettina

Bettina, pregnant with his child, survived the crash, but Aly and his unborn child did not.

He was forty-eight.

Book 3

Beginning of An End

Chapter One: K

In 1936, the Spanish Civil War broke out, King Edward VIII abdicated the British throne, Charlie Chaplin released his iconic film, Modern Times, and Shah Karim Al Hussaini, Aga Khan IV, was born in Geneva, Switzerland.

Known as "K" to his friends, he was born to Prince Alykhan and Joan Guinness on December 13, 1936. His birth, however, raised many eyebrows, as it occurred just seven months after his parents' marriage.

His mother, Joan Guinness, renamed *Tajudwallah*, had been convicted of adultery with his father, Prince Aly Khan, at the Ritz Hotel earlier that same year.

During World War II, K and his younger brother, Amyn, spent their early childhood in Kenya before being sent to Switzerland to study at Le Rosey School in Gstaad, Switzerland.

Later, K pursued Islamic History at Harvard University in the United States, where he shared a room with Pierre Trudeau, who would later become the Prime Minister of Canada.

While still at university, on 11 July 1957, SMS, his grandfather, Aga Khan III passed away, designating K as the forty-ninth Imam of the Nizari Ismailis and Aga Khan IV.

Takhat Nashini (ascension to the throne)

On 19 October of the same year, K's *Takhat Nashini* (ascension to the throne) ceremonies began in Dar-es-Salaam, followed by Nairobi.

Willi Frischauer, the biographer of SMS, captured the scene in his book, *The Aga Khans:*

"On a smaller scale, the Nairobi Takhat Nashini was a repetition of the Dar-es-Salaam ceremony. In the grounds of the Aga Khan Club, the lone figure of the young new leader seated high on the throne amid his people was strangely appealing. The red robes and gold turbans of the Ismaili dignitaries, who invested him with robe, pagri, sword, chain, and ring, created a vivid picture like Kenya had never seen before. The dias, a mass of flowers red, blue, white, and yellow stood out against the backdrop of flags fluttering gently in the slight breeze. A thousand people of all races gathered for the social event that evening to greet the Aga Khan, who arrived with the Governor of Kenya, Sir Evelyn Baring. There was dancing to the regimental band's music and a sumptuous dinner."

The third ceremony was held in Kampala on 25 October 1957, before moving on to Karachi, where 150,000 followers and dignitaries gathered to mark the occasion.

Takht Nashini (ascension to the throne) ceremony

Willi Frischauer described the scene:

"The sound of trumpets heralded the arrival of the Aga Khan, accompanied by Pakistan's President. Prime Minister Malik Firoz Khan Noon and his cabinet were already seated. The brief act of installation mirrored the East African ritual, except for the presentation of a rare, three-hundred-year-old copy of the Holy Quran an exquisite example of Arab calligraphy. It had been written in Medina by a Haji from Bokhara."

The fourth ceremony took place in Dacca on 12 February 1958, followed by the final one in Bombay on 11 March 1958.

During his reign, K left an indelible mark on the world stage, earning global recognition as a horse breeder, business magnate, and a humanitarian.

His achievements were acknowledged with numerous accolades. Yet, the pinnacle of his legacy lies in the founding of Aga Khan Development Network (AKDN), one of the world's largest privately owned humanitarian organizations.

But K's life was an extraordinary paradox!!

He was a hedonistic billionaire, living a royal existence in a palace in Portugal. On one hand, he was a revered spiritual leader; on the other, a charlatan. He owned jets, yachts, private islands, and a vast business empire, all while claiming to live on a modest budget. He was both a convicted adulterer and a figure who instigated his divinity behind the closed doors of *Jamatkhanas*.

Agakhan IV

Islamic Cult

Cults often emerge as offshoots of mainstream religions such as Christianity and Hinduism. After all, both embraced the concept of a God in human form.

In the twentieth century, the world witnessed the rise and fall of numerous cult leaders and movements stemming from Christian ideology, including figures like Jim Jones and David Koresh.

In the Hindu community, leaders such as Gurmeet Ram Rahim, Nithyananda, and Asaram Bapu have come to exemplify the rise of godmen who also became cult figures.

In contrast, Islam rejects the notion of anyone, or anything being considered divine besides God. It is no wonder, therefore, that historically Islam did not develop cults…except Agakhanism!!

While the definition of a cult remains a subject of debate, it can generally be understood as a group led by a charismatic leader who manipulates followers through charm, indoctrination, or other psychological tactics for personal gain.

Members of such groups are required to adhere to a strict set of rituals and practices, and, most crucially, offer unwavering devotion to the leader. Failure to comply often results in excommunication and ostracism, the draconian nature of which we shall discuss in further detail later in this work.

Incidentally, Agakhanism ticks all the boxes!

Whilst K claimed to be a Shia Muslim Imam, his conduct and operations, did not resemble the Prophet of Islam or his alleged ancestor *Mawla Ali*.

Rather, it bears a striking similarity to late Shri Sathya Sai Baba…. a Hindu cult leader of international repute!

Shri Satya Sai Baba

Sathyanarayana Raju was born on November 23, 1926, in the village of Puttaparthi in Andhra Pradesh. He earned a reputation early in life for being 'unusually intelligent,' spiritual, and capable of performing miraculous feats, such as materializing sweets out of thin air for children.

It wasn't long before people began showering divine attributes to the young boy, a natural response in a culture where miracles are often linked to divinity.

In 1940, at the age of fourteen, he declared himself the reincarnation of Shirdi Sai Baba, a globally revered saint. Over time, he solidified his claim by performing 'miracles' that further convinced his followers. Among these was a notable feat where he regurgitated a golden egg in front of thousands and produced *vibhuti* (sacred ash) seemingly from nowhere.

And so, he became the new Sai Baba…Shri Satya Sai Baba.

In 1972, Baba founded the Sri Sathya Sai Central Trust to enable its members to undertake human service as a path to spiritual advancement.

He built a network of free hospitals, medical clinics, drinking water projects, schools, universities, ashrams, auditoriums, and educational initiatives.

Over time, he became a guru of global renown, overseeing 2,000 Sai Centers in 137 countries and earning the devotion of tens of millions.

Among his followers were prominent figures such as Indian Prime Minister Manmohan Singh, Congress President Sonia Gandhi, Gujarat Chief Minister Narendra Modi (the current Prime Minister), cricketer Sachin Tendulkar.

Baba passed away on April 24, 2011, at his hospital from multiple organ failure. His funeral was attended by both local and international dignitaries, and he was laid to rest with full state honors.

His universal message *"Love All, Serve All"* and *"Help Ever, Hurt Never"* resonated deeply.

While there's no doubt Baba's philanthropy and influence reached far and wide, there was also a…dark side!!

Accusations of trickery, sexual abuse, money laundering, and fraud ran parallel to Baba's humanitarian and spiritual projects.

The first glimpse into this darker side emerged in 1963, when Baba suffered a stroke and four consecutive heart attacks, leaving him partially paralyzed. Yet, in a spectacle witnessed by thousands, he "miraculously" healed the paralysis.

Many were skeptical…for two key reasons: First, the paralysis could have been faked and second, Baba chose to heal himself in a public gathering rather than in the privacy of a hospital.

In 2003, suspicions found firmer ground when Baba slipped from a stool and broke his hip. This time however there was no miracle! Only a wheelchair could provide him with mobility until his death.

Before that episode, beginning in 1972, rationalists had begun challenging Baba's miraculous powers. Among them, the most discomforting challenge came from Hossur Narasimhaiah, a physicist, rationalist, and then vice-chancellor of Bangalore University. He dared Baba to perform his miracles under controlled conditions.

Baba ignored him but not without consequences!

Not only did it harm Baba's popularity, but it also led to accusations of trickery and sleight of hand from both local and international media. As if that weren't enough, Alaya Rahm, a former devotee of Baba, accused him of sexual abuse on live television.

After Baba's death, more scrutiny followed, particularly regarding his handling of money. On June 17, 2011, officials from the Sri Sathya Sai Central Trust opened his sealed residence, accompanied by government and bank officials. Inside, they discovered nearly 100 kilograms of gold ornaments, 307 kilograms of silver ornaments, and Rs 116 million in cash—donated by devotees from around the world.

Despite the negative publicity since, Baba remains a revered figure to this day!!

Throughout my research on Baba and K, I found striking similarities!

Both were spiritual leaders, followed by millions and engaged in humanitarian efforts. Both used deceptions to extort reverence, money, and jewelry. Both were non-transparent and accused of sexual misconduct. Both were challenged by rationalists, Baba by Hossur Narasimhaiah, while K was confronted by me. My interactions with K have been elaborated later in this work.

In any case, K and Baba also shared dissimilarities.

K's divinity was confined behind the closed doors of *Jamatkhana* and the obscurity of *ginans,* while Baba was vocal about his claims of divinity. Furthermore, K deceived the global public into funding humanitarian agencies, which generated profits through development services. In contrast, Baba's Sai Trust genuinely offered free healthcare, education, food, water, clothing, and electricity to the needy.

K and his women

The pattern of woman chasing and divorcing was a tradition within the Aga Khan dynasty. SMS's abandonment of his first wife, Shahzadi, followed by divorce from his third wife, Andree Carron, in 1943 are well documented.

K's father Alykhan's life was also marred by familial disasters. He was divorced by his first wife, Joan Guinness, and later by his second wife, film star Rita Hayworth, both unable to tolerate his promiscuity.

Similarly, K's uncle, Sadri, divorced his wife, Nina Dyer, in 1962, a year before her tragic suicide.

K continued this family tradition.

Annouchka

In 1959, twenty-three-year-old, spiritual leader of Nizari Ismailis visited a St. Tropez nightclub. Soon a sixteen-year-old blue-eyed blonde Annouchka von Menks caught his eye!!

In a style reminiscent of his father, Aly the Casanova, he approached her and introduced himself:

"I'm the Aga Khan," he said.

Initially, the teenager thought it was funny. She had seen pictures of the Aga Khan in the papers and recalled he was an old man with a walking stick. Here was a young man claiming to be Aga Khan, the celebrity!!

Then a friend whispered in her ear that the old Aga Khan was dead.

Once Annouchka recovered from her shock, she apologized. Before departing, they agreed to have lunch the next day.

An affair had begun.

Both, however, viewed it with contrasting intentions.

She was hoping to one day drag him to the altar, while K had "other" plans!!

He once told media concerning marrying Annouchka:

Just because I date a girl doesn't mean I am on the verge of matrimony, ".

K with Annouchka

Soon, there was a new girl in his life!

Dolores

Dolores von Furstenberg Guinness was a relative of K's mother's first husband, Thomas Guiness. They were inseparable for almost a year.

Young Annouchka, on the other hand gave birth to K's child in Neuilly, a suburb of Paris.

Then both women disappeared from the headlines…for good!!

Sally

As a young man, K had a few flings such as Anouchka and Dolores, but eventually he married a British model, Sally Croker-Poole, officially known as the Begum Salimah Aga Khan.

Despite warnings of his infidelities, she was seduced by his courtship and lavish gifts of expensive jewelry. Perhaps shaped by her own experience with failed relationships, she accepted his proposal and converted to Islam.

Their marriage produced three children: Princess Zahra, Prince Rahim (the current Aga khan), and Prince Hussain.

Sally

Although the Begum was aware of K's past, she remained utterly oblivious to his present… her husband was involved in extramarital affairs.

Three women emerged in particular: the Italian beauty Milena Maffei, a jewelry shop owner; Ariane Soldati; and Pilar Goess, an Austrian nude model for Playboy magazine.

Begum once remarked, *"Milena is always shadowing me! Whenever I go to the races, she's just a few yards away."*

As for Pilar, Begum is reported to have said,

"What I particularly disliked about her—apart from her being with my husband—was how she integrated my children into the affair. K and Pilar would walk along the Bois de Boulogne with my sons in tow. She appeared frequently on his yacht, lavishing attention on the boys. Rahim and Hussain were flattered by her affection. She would read to them and care for them."

Eventually, Begum left the family home and sought a divorce. The case was settled in 1995, with reports alleging that the Begum received twenty million pounds and seventeen million pounds in jewelry.

Following the divorce, K remained single for the next three years.

Gabriele

In 1998, K met Gabriele Zu Leiningen, a London-based lawyer and entertainer. A romance soon blossomed, culminating in marriage.

She was twenty-six years his junior.

Gabrielle

Soon she adopted an Islamic name Begum Inaara and a couple of years later gave birth to a son, Aly Mohammad.

However, it didn't take long for K to lose interest in his new wife. A close friend shared his experiences with the German newspaper *Bild.*

"At first, he [K] couldn't keep his hands off her. No gift was too expensive. But once his enthusiasm wanes, his heart turns to ice."

Six years into their marriage, the new Begum learned that her sixty-eight-year-old husband had been having an affair with a flight attendant!!

Armed with evidence gathered by private detectives, she initiated divorce proceedings. A Paris Court of Appeal eventually helped negotiate a £54 million settlement.

The high society saw the settlement as a 'bargain.'

I was a devoted follower during both divorces of my then spiritual father. I remember being told by the system that these divorces had stemmed from our Imam's neglect of his own family in favor of nurturing his spiritual children.

Being a victim of blind faith at the time, I remember shedding a few tears!!

Yet, the pattern of failed marriages within the dynasty continued.

In recent times, women jumped into the ring, starting with K's stepsister, Yasmin, whose marriage collapsed first with Basil Embiricos, and then with Christopher Jeffries. Next, K's daughter, Zahra, parted ways with her husband, Mark Bowden.

Then the boys joined the circus!

K's younger son, Hussain, split from his wife, Kristin White, renamed Khaliya, in 2011. He later married Elizabeth Hoag, a mental health counselor from Connecticut. She was renamed Fareen.

Khaliya

Then his elder brother Rahim, now the 50th Nizari Imam, and Agakhan V, ended his marriage to the American model, Kendra Spears.

Mata Salamat Kendra Spears

One dynasty, three generations, eleven marriages… a 100% divorce rate!!

For over a century, the *Noorani* family has struggled to keep their family intact. A stark contrast to the belief held by his followers that their Imam is a *Mushkil Kusha*, a "Destroyer of Difficulties."

Mushkil Kusha

Majalises (religious gatherings) are a daily occurrence in the *Jamatkhanas* around the world, yet there is one significant gathering that takes place every six months.

This special event is dedicated to holding prayers aimed at resolving severe personal or familial challenges and calamities such as wars or natural disasters. The prayers to the Imam, are known as *Satado*—the "seven days" of intense supplication.

Believers collectively pray to the Imam for resolution of their difficulties.

One might wonder what qualification did K have to rid people of their difficulties?

The answer lies in Shia history.

Mawla Ali, the first Shia Imam, stands at the center of every Shia Muslim's religious universe. Islamic history is rich with stories of Mawla Ali's gallantry and his pivotal role in establishing Islam.

One such legend recounts the conquest of Khyber, a fortified Jewish town, during which the Islamic army was on the brink of retreat.

Despite the Prophet's leadership and relentless efforts, after twenty days of failed attempts, the town remained impenetrable. It was only then that the Prophet called for Mawla Ali, who, despite suffering from a debilitating eye infection, led the charge and conquered the fort.

Thenceforth, Mawla Ali earned the revered title of *Mushkil Kusha* "destroyer of difficulties." Hence, as an alleged descendant of Mawla Ali, his followers invoked K in times of hardship.

Yet K's ability to resolve difficulties had never been tested… until 1972.

Ugandan Crisis

In the late nineteenth century, many Asians migrated to East Africa, where they settled and became British subjects. Known for their business acumen and entrepreneurial spirit, they thrived financially. This made them the target of envy among the indigenous communities, particularly in Uganda.

By 1962, the Ugandan Prime Minister, Milton Obote, had begun a policy that came to be known as Africanization, which many considered a form of ethnic cleansing aimed at the Asian population.

A decade later, this policy escalated into a humanitarian disaster, orchestrated by the brutal dictator Idi Amin Dada.

Amin, who had 'won' the presidency in a coup in 1971, harbored ambitions to "cleanse" Uganda of its Asian

Indians fleeing Uganda in 1972

population, drawing a disturbing parallel to Hitler's actions during the Holocaust.

While timely intervention by the United Nations prevented a full-scale genocide, it did nothing to stop Amin's decision to expel the Asians from Uganda.

In 1972, Amin gave the Asian community just three months to leave. During this time, he oversaw the looting of their businesses and homes, among other atrocities. Traumatized and displaced, many Asians fled Uganda, resettling in various parts of the world.

Among the refugees were a few thousand followers of K, who were fortunate to have a living Imam, the *Mushkil Kusha,* their protecter.

K rose to the occasion.

He called Pierre Trudeau, the Canadian Prime Minister and a former roommate from his Harvard days. Special visas for his distressed followers were issued and K sent planes to bring them to their new home…Canada.

This was nothing short of a miracle for his followers!

Their faith in K grew stronger than ever. The story of Uganda is still told with pride within the community.

But then a question arose albeit outside the Nizari Ismaili bubble:

Why did K not display those divine powers the previous year, in 1971, when thousands of his devotees perished during the Bangla Crisis?

Bangla Crisis

In 1947, before leaving, the British divided India. Pakistan was born as a republic which was split into two geographical regions: East and West Pakistan.

Yet, to the envy and resentment of the East, West Pakistan held far more political and economic power. This led to a separatist movement in the East, known as the Bangladesh Liberation War.

To suppress the uprising, West Pakistan, under the leadership of President Yahya Khan launched Operation Searchlight on the night of March 25, 1971, resulting in a brutal genocide.

Among those affected were K's disciples, including members of my wife's family. The homeless, traumatized, and distressed followers crossed the border from East Pakistan into India on foot. Many made it while others were not so lucky.

Bengalis fleeing the genocide

Question endures: *Where was K, the Mushkil Kusha?*

Not only was he absent in Bangladesh but few decades later, in Afghanistan, where his followers faced a catastrophe!!

War On Terror

In 2001, K was presented with another opportunity to protect his spiritual children.

That year, geo-political and religious tensions between Islam and Western nations reached a breaking point.

The world will forever remember the disaster that followed: the 9/11 terrorist attacks on the United States. Passenger planes were hijacked and flown into landmarks in United States including the Twin Towers in New York, claiming thousands of lives.

Al-Qaeda, a terrorist organization based in Afghanistan and led by Osama Bin Laden, took responsibility. In response, the U.S. government declared a war on terrorism and invaded Afghanistan. By the time the mission concluded thirteen years later, over 200,000 Afghans had perished.

Among the dead were Hazara Ismailis, K's followers, who were left homeless, maimed, raped, and killed.

But there was no *Mushkil Kusha* nor his planes!!

Terrorized Afghan children during war on terror

Syrian Civil War

For decades, the Assad dynasty in Syria had ruled with an iron fist. In March 2011, widespread discontent with Bashar al-Assad's government sparked large-scale protests and pro-democracy rallies across Syria. The movement quickly gained global momentum, with participants from around the world joining in opposition to the regime's brutality.

By 2012, the rallies had escalated into a full-blown civil war. Tens of thousands of Syrians, including K's followers, endured torture and brutal killings. In 2015, a rocket attack on Hama killed eleven Ismailis.

Then, in 2016, the ARA News Agency of Syria reported that ISIS had threatened the Ismailis of Salamiya to either surrender or face the consequences.

Civilians fleeing the Syrian civil war in 2011

In response, Ismaili cleric Haider al-Salef made a desperate appeal to the international community for protection.

The international community did not intervene!

K, the *Mushkil Kusha*, on the other hand committed $50 million for rebuild Syria and mobilized his humanitarian agency FOCUS on the ground.

However, as time would reveal, neither K's planes nor the promised $50 million ever materialized—and FOCUS was unable to save the lives of the desperate Ismailis pleading for help."

Yours Affectionately

The *Mushkil Kusha* had failed, but does that mean he didn't love his spiritual children?

If he didn't, then why would he conclude every *taliqa* (a written message) to his disciples with *"Yours affectionately, Aga Khan"*?

In 1979, this relationship of love and affection was put to the test.

The place was Sydney, Australia. At the time, the *jamaat* in Australia was still in its infancy, with fewer than a hundred devotees.

Ritualistically, they had prayed all their lives for K's *deedar* (a physical sighting). However, deep down, they knew their chances were almost nil, especially since larger *jamaats* worldwide were struggling to receive it.

Then, a miracle happened!

K was coming to Sydney!

The Australian *jamaat* could scarcely believe their good fortune. The news was met with celebration: a congregational dinner and *dandiya* (a traditional Gujarati folk dance)

On November 7, 1979, K, the God arrived with Goddess, Begum Salimah in Sydney.

His arrival was seen as confirmation of the belief that no prayer goes unheard. The devotees pinched themselves, hardly able to grasp the reality of the moment.

Then the good fortune got better!!

The divine couple shared a meal with them, something K rarely did when meeting his spiritual children.

Then, as quickly as they had arrived, they left, leaving Sydney *Jamat* in tears.

But the miracles didn't stop there!!

Eight years later, in 1987…. K reappeared!

I was among the devotees who considered himself the luckiest man on earth. Not only to receive the *deedar,* but to be given an opportunity to carry the luggage from his private jet and deliver it to the Sydney Intercontinental Hotel.

The devotees were over the moon. Then it was time for him to depart.

Although we had been fortunate enough to have been blessed with his *deedar* twice in eight years, the *jamaat* continued to pray for more, as it does to the day.

But then the prayers stopped working, just like a cheap copy of a watch!!

K would never come to Australia!!

So, what went wrong? Why wouldn't the all-knowing hear the Australian *Jamaat's* prayers anymore?

As I learned later, in 1979, he had never intended to travel to Australia to meet his spiritual children. Rather, he had accepted an invitation from the Victoria Racing Club to be their guest speaker for the upcoming Spring Carnival in Melbourne. Sydney conveniently happened to be a couple of hours away.

Again, in 1987, K's yacht Azzurra, participated in the America's Cup in Fremantle, Western Australia. Unfortunately, it lost to the American challenger Stars & Stripes 87.

K was in Perth to watch the event and again Sydney was close by!!

Chapter 2

Spiritual Deception

Descendant of the Prophet

In the introduction, we discussed that K had ordained an Ismaili Constitution in 1986 to declare himself the descendant of the Prophet through Mawla Ali and his daughter Fatima.

The long journey of K's spiritual deception starts here. To comprehend it, we must cast an eye on the following verse of the Holy Quran.

"It is He Who created you from a single person, and made his mate of like nature, in order that he might dwell with her in love"

Surah Al Araf: Ayat 189

In the Holy Quran, Allah refers to a single person, Adam, the *Abu Bashar*, the father of mankind. Therefore, in Islam, descent is determined by the male issue rather than female.

Fo Aga khan to claim descent from the Prophet is not only absurd but deceptive because the prophet did not leave a progeny. Although, he had three sons, named Abd Allah, Ibrahim, and Qasim, tragically, none of them survived to advance his progeny.

Christian Trinity

Whenever K met or wrote to his followers, he referred to them as "my beloved spiritual children"

Islam views spiritual relationship as one that exists between a supernatural being, the almighty Allah and his mortal creation.

Christianity, another monotheistic religion, however, attempts to fuse the person of a mortal (Jesus)with God, his creator. The idea of Trinity asserts that three persons, Father (God), son (Jesus), the Holy Ghost, share one essence.

Agakhanism, although, claiming to belong to the Islamic fold, fuses Christian ideology with Hindu Gods to explain the fundamental question of our relationship with Allah.

A *ginan,* provides a glaring but disturbing evidence of this Islamic blasphemy by depicting the Nizari Imam as the manifestation of a trinity of Hindu Gods.

Ejee bhrahmaa veeshnav maheshar bhanneeye

Kal maa(n)he veeshnu(n) Imaam

Meaning

Knowing Brahma, Vishnu and Mahesh. In the present age Lord Vishnu is the Imam.

Shirk (associating partners with Allah)

The Islamic concept of Tawhid, the absolute oneness of God is the bedrock of Islam, a doctrine upon which the entire structure of the faith rests.

The Holy Qur'an is unequivocal on the concept of God.

God neither begets nor is begotten (Surah Ikhlas Ayat 3)

To submit to God, every Muslim must recite the *shahada* (declaration of faith) that affirms this oneness.

Ašhadu 'al lā ilāha illa l-Lāh, wa 'ašhadu 'anna muḥammadar rasūlu l-Lāh.

Meaning

I testify that there is no God except Allah, and that Muhammad is Allah's messenger.

Shia Muslims owing to their veneration for Mawla Ali, include him in their *shahada* as a vice regent of Allah.

Ašhadu 'al lā ilāha illa l-Lāh, wa 'ašhadu 'anna muḥammadar rasūlu l-Lāh wa ashahadu 'anna 'Aliyyan waliyyu l-Lāh.

Meaning

I testify that there is no God except Allah, and that Muhammad is Allah's messenger. I testify that Ali is the vicegerent of Allah.

Agakhanism, on its part also includes Malwa Ali and hence the present Imam in the *shahada.* However, unlike Shia Muslims, with the deployment of an ambiguous term, the identity of their Imam converges with Allah.

Ašhadu 'al lā ilāha illa l-Lāh, wa 'ašhadu 'anna muḥammadar rasūlu l-Lāh, Ašhaduan Aliyun amirul momineen alyullah

Meaning

"I testify that there is no god but Allah, and that Muhammad is Allah's messenger. I testify that Ali is the leader of the believers, who is either from Allah or is Allah."

The ambiguity lies in the term...*Aliyullah.*

It can mean Ali is from Allah or that Ali is Allah.

If interpreted as Ali is from Allah, the claim at worst would be debatable. However, if it is understood as Ali is Allah, it becomes an act of *Shirk,* the gravest sin of associating partners with Allah.

The central question arises:

How do followers of Agakhan interpret the controversial term, *Aliyullah*?

Do they believe Ali is from Allah or Ali is Allah?

The answer lies behind the closed-door of the *Jamatkhana* where their prayers, rituals and ceremonies scream aloud relentlessly…. **Ali is Allah!!**

Dua

The Aga Khan prayer is known as Dua. Each of its six parts begin with a verse from the holy Quran and conclude with prostration and submission to Allah. However, the design of the Dua serves an ulterior purpose.

To merge the authority of the Prophet and the attributes of Allah with the figure of their Imam.

The deception is achieved with the use of ambiguity, assigning multiple Islamic identities to their Imam, leveraging upon and distorting various historical situations and most disturbingly.........redacting a verse of the Holy Quran!!

*S*urah *Fateha* is affectionately known as *Ummul Qur'an* in the Islamic world. Muslims of all denominations around the world recite this *Surah* daily, considering it obligatory in their prayers.

During recitation of one of its verses, they declare:

You ˹alone˺ we worship and You ˹alone˺ we ask for help (Surah Fateha Ayat 5)

Agakhanis, like all Muslims recite this verse in their Dua, however it does'nt long take before they contradict it. In the same prayer, they declare:

Seek, at times of difficulty, the help of your Lord, the present living Imam Shah Rahim al-Husayni.

The Holy Quran commands believers to send salutations to the Prophet.

"Allah and His Angels send Salat upon the Prophet. O you who believe, ask [Allah] to confer Salat upon him, and greet him with a thorough salutation."

Surah Al-Ahzab, Ayah 56

It is important to note that this honor of being saluted is exclusively bestowed upon Prophet Muhammad despite the presence of Mawla Ali at the time.

Notwithstanding, the Agakhan Dua includes not only Mawla Ali but his progeny, including Rahim, the present Imam as worthy of salutations!!

O Allah, let Thy peace be upon Muhammad, the Chosen, and upon 'Aly, the Favorite, and upon the Imams, the Pure, and the Evidence of Thy Authority, the Lord of the Age and Time, our present living Imam, Mawlana Shah Rahim il Husayni.

The salutation however serves another purpose! It introduces the Imam as *Hujjat ul-Amr* the "Evidence of God's authority on earth"

Redaction of the Holy Verse

To give firm ground to the Imam's self-proclamation as a *Hujjat ul-Amr* the "Evidence of God's authority on earth", the Dua features a verse of the Holy Scripture to assign the Imam yet another identity… *Ulil Amr, or "holder of authority."*

"O ye, who believe, obey Allah, and obey the Apostle and holders of authority from amongst you."

Sura Nisa, Ayat 59

The believers meanwhile remain oblivious to the fact that *Ulil Amr* has a historical context unrelated to Mawla Ali or his progeny.

In the same section, the Agakhan Dua, features yet another verse of the Holy Quran!!

"And We have vested everything in the manifest Imam."

Sura Yaseen, Redacted Ayat 12

This time the prayer assigns the Imam a new and distinct identity: *Imam e-Mubeen,* the "manifest Imam"

However, the verse is redacted!!

If the verse were recited in its entirety, the true meaning would be revealed, one that excludes Nizari Imam or any living person, from being the *Imam e-Mubeen*.

It reads:

"Verily, we give life to the dead, and We record that which they have sent before and that which they leave behind; and We have encompassed everything in a clear Book (Imam)."

Sura Yaseen, Ayah 12

This verse serves as a reminder of the past which is meticulously recorded in a clear Book of evidence.

Importantly, the term Imam in this context does not refer to the Shia Imams, nor any specific individual, rather a book of records.

Mukhi plays the Prophet

In *Surah Fatah*, Allah authorizes the Prophet to accept an oath of allegiance on His behalf from the believers.

(O Prophet) Verily, those who give Thee their allegiance, they give it but to Allah (Himself); Allah's hand is upon their hands. Then he who breaks it, certainly breaks

it against himself. And he who fulfills what he has pledged with Allah shall be rewarded with an abundant recompense. Sura Fatah, Ayat 10

In *Jamatkhanas* around the world, the same scenario is enacted daily except.... The characters differ!!

Allah is personified by Rahim, the current Imam and the Prophet by his *Mukhi*!!

The believers queue up to offer their allegiance to the Mukhi on behalf of the Imam!!

(Entire Dua is provided in the appendix)

Mazhar (Manifestation) of Allah

As previously discussed in this chapter, K strategically invoked the Holy Quran to reinforce his pursuit of divine authority.

Accordingly, the design of the Dua assigned him numerous divine as well as mortal identities.

This led to confusion amongst critical thinkers in the global *Jamaat*.

What was his real identity after all? They wondered.

Recognizing the potential for discord, K decided it was wise to extinguish the growing tensions before they turned into a fire. He convened a meeting with the global leadership of the Ismaili Association.

This gathering became known as the Paris Conference of 1975.

The purpose of the conference was to clarify his identity.

While K acknowledged the absolute transcendence of God, he once again engaged in the traditional game of hide and seek concerning his own identity.

He suggested that the Imam could be understood by the believer as the "*Mazhar (manifestation) of Allah*"

Concerning his relationship with Allah, he suggested:

The relationship between God and Imam is characterized by varying levels of inspiration and communication from God to man.

His identity had just become more ambiguous than it was!!

The suggestion that the Imam was both a manifestation of God and an intermediary at the same time was raised. Though these ideas seem absurd, it sparks a fundamental question:

Did Islam ever embrace the concept of a Mazhar, or divine manifestation?

The answer lies in the Holy Qur'an.

His light is illustrated with the example of a niche containing a lamp, which is encased in glass, as if it were a pearly star, lit by the oil of a blessed olive tree, neither from the east nor the west, whose oil would almost glow even without fire. Light upon light. Allah guides to His light whom He will. And Allah presents examples for people, for He is Knowledgeable of all things

Sura An-Nur, Ayat 35

The Holy text confirms that God's light manifests, but does this mean it manifests in human form? This question was also answered in another verse:

He did not beget, nor was He begotten (Sura Ikhlas, Ayat 3)

It is for this reason, the idea of anything or anyone including a Shia Imam as the manifestation of God lies outside the bounds of Islam.

K had committed *Shirk*.... not only verbally but in writing!

(an excerpt of the Paris Conference report can be found in the appendix)

Life Magazine

In 1983, K's conflicting identities were unintentionally brought into the public spotlight by a December issue of Life magazine.

It introduced him as:

"To 15 million Muslims in 25 countries, he is a living god, a direct descendant of Mohammed, and the spokesman for almighty Allah."

Sensing potential Muslim backlash, K's Secretariat issued a communique which was subsequently published in the February 1984 issue of Life.

"The Aga Khan is the 49th hereditary Imam the spiritual leader of the Shia Imami Ismaili Muslims. The unity

of Allah, Tawheed, is one of the fundamental principles of Islam. For Life to assert that the Aga Khan is 'a living god' and 'a spokesman for Allah' is a complete misrepresentation of the most basic tenet of one of the world's major faiths and a serious affront to all Muslims."

Life magazine apologized.... blissfully unaware that the apology was not warranted!! K was in fact being revered as God in a bubble of iron called *Jamatkhana.*

Life had been deceived and so was the Muslim Ummah!!

But for K, it was just another day at the office!

Copyright Affair

In 2010, K finally revealed his identity!!

Out of reverence for him, his Canadian followers Alnaz Jiwa and Nagib Tajdin set out to compile his *farmans* and distribute them to spread his teachings.

However, this activity was considered a violation of the Ismaili Constitution by the local leadership. After all, the *farmans* were K's intellectual property, and he had entrusted their publication to his institution, the Ismaili Tariqah &

Religious Education Board (ITREB), formerly Ismaili Association.

As a result, the duo was ordered by the leadership to cease their distribution, as it represented a breach of copyright.

However, Jiwa and Tajdin displayed extra ordinary courage and resolve …. They defied the order!!

It is unclear whether they were aware that defying the order meant challenging the Imam, which could result in the horrors of ex-communication.

After several episodes of verbal confrontations and a prolonged battle of egos, both parties found themselves in the Supreme Court of Canada.

K initiated legal proceedings for breach of copyright and successfully sued the duo. The court ordered all stock to be recalled.

K had won the case, but in doing so, he had essentially driven a nail into his own coffin.

The Nizari global community, especially in Canada, had been closely following the copyright drama. Through the ordeal, their Imam had clearly revealed his avarice, a stark contrast to his supposed spiritual claims.

But did this revelation stop his followers, including *Jiwa and Tajdin* from revering K or from attending the *Jamatkhana*?

Not in the slightest.

As mind-boggling as it may seem, despite K's exposure as a charlatan, it was business as usual.

But how is this possible?

Willing Blindness

At this point, it's important to understand the composition of the community from socio-economic, cultural, and psychological perspectives.

As mentioned earlier, Nizari Ismailis are made of two groups: Original Ismailis from western and central Asia and the *Khojas* of Indian origin. The former belongs to lower- or middle-class socio- economic backgrounds, often out of touch with the broader picture. Just as their lives are shaped by simplicity, their religious beliefs, passed down through centuries, remain grounded in blind faith and tradition.

The *Khojas*, in contrast, present a minority within the community. Avaricious, highly educated, and typically belong to the middle or upper socio-economic classes, they are well-positioned in leadership roles.

Despite their minority status, *Khojas* can be categorized into three groups based on their *Jamatkhana* attendance and the strength of their religious convictions, or the lack thereof.

The first group consists of fanatics, whose devotion leaves no room for reason. To them, K is infallible, and any further discussion ends there. Within this group, there is a sub-set of individuals who go out of their way to showcase both their religious knowledge and their devotion. Both sub-groups attend Jamatkhana regularly, though they represent less than 10% of K's followers.

Next following consists of politicians and aspiring politicians. The leadership structure is vast, comprising numerous religious and non-religious institutions, as well as an enormous army of volunteers running the cult on behalf of K. Their attendance at the *Jamatkhana* largely depends on the responsibilities associated with their position. This group make up approximately 25% of the global jamaat.

Lastly, as per SMS's design, the largest group of *Khoja* attendees consists of clubbers and socializers who view the *Jamatkhana* as little more than a weekend outing.

For them, the social aspect takes precedence over the spiritual and doctrinal aspects of the system.

When controversies such as accusations of adultery, money laundering, or lawsuits against their Imam arise, their immediate and instinctive reaction is to bury their heads in the sand. Not only to avoid the system's heavy-handed tactics but to ensure the continued existence of social and political club…. near and dear to their hearts.

It is this very willing blindness that allows the followers of Aga khan to justify the ignorance of their faith, indifference towards the practice of Islamic blasphemy and acceptance of criminal activities in the place of worship.

Chapter Three

The Spiritual Franchise

The world had changed between life and times of SMS and the era in which K ruled the hearts and pockets of his followers.

It was more materialistic!!

K had inherited a business generating hundreds of millions annually selling spiritual ideas and services such as *dasond, mehmani* (cash gifts), food and jewelry auctions, majlis membership fees, and a plethora of revenue attracting rituals and ceremonies.

As they say, greed has no boundaries!

K wanted more and to get it he not only improvised the inheritance but revolutionized it!!

He transformed the cult into a global franchise where he was the franchisor and the sole financial beneficiary of the revenue.

The globe was split into territories based on geography. Each territory represented by a council (his own appointee) was given franchisee rights. In turn, the franchisees would operate a set number of stores called *Jamatkhanas* in their respective jurisdictions trading spiritual services and creative ideas to generate revenue.

Then K made a discovery!!

It was about to multiply his already colossal takings many times over!!

Four clubs and four heavens

As discussed earlier, SMS had created an elite class within the *Jamaatkhana* by establishing a leadership hierarchy. This leadership gave of their time and skills to help him amass wealth. In fact, they personally funded the operations in return for social prestige in the community.

However, what SMS, the genius had overlooked was a class of wealthy individuals who did not wish to give of their time and skills…. but had a need to be important and rub shoulders with the elites.

It took the ingenuity of K to discover the niche!!

The targeted spiritual children wanted to be elites without spending time, albeit they were happy to spend money.

Eureka! The idea of spiritual clubs was born.

To cater to each according to his wealth, four secretive, exclusive, and supposedly spiritual *majlises* were established. Each would command a progressively higher membership fee, accompanied by corresponding levels of prestige, fashion, glitter, and, occasionally, some skin.

Club One: Life Dedication

Eji kaho re jeev tame kis karan aavya...Na kidhi sahebji ni sreva?

Meaning

Tell me O brother, what purpose did you serve as a human, if you did'nt serve the Imam?

The *ginans,* had always emphasized that serving the Imam is the true purpose of one's life. This idea became the foundation of the first exclusive "spiritual" club.

K made a *Farman*, explaining its significance. Its gist was along the lines of:

Throughout Ismaili history a band of disciples had lived with the Imam of the time or remained close to him, assisting with chores and specific tasks. In the modern age, such direct service was no longer possible due to geography. But how could he, as their Imam, deprive his followers of the opportunity to serve him? Thus, out of his 'love' for them, he graciously allowed his disciples to serve him symbolically by joining the Life Dedication majlis.

Membership would symbolically mean a lifetime of service to the Imam, which was marketed as one way ticket to heaven!!

Socializing and prestige in this life and heaven in the next. All of this, for a membership fee and the repetition of the money-attracting rituals of daily *Jamatkhana* and various *majalises.*

It was no brainer for the wealthy!

For K, the exclusivity of Life had created another favorable situation. The middle class yearned to be included in the exclusive club. They began cutting corners to afford the extra expense.

The lower class missed out.... but then such was Life!!

Club Two: Fidai

As discussed in earlier chapters, *Hassan ibn Sabbah,* the eleventh century Nizari Ismaili *da'i*, had inspired his followers *(Fidayeen or Assasins)* to kill and be killed for the Nizari movement, promising them free entry into heaven.

The Assasin legacy gave K the inspiration for his next spiritual club.

He appropriately named it, *Fidai Majlis* and made a *Farman*, explaining its significance. Its gist was along the lines of:

Throughout Ismaili history a band of very special disciples were chosen to carry out tasks which involved risk of life. In modern times, however, such activities have become redundant. But how could he, the current Imam, deprive his followers of missing out on the opportunity of dying for him? Thus, out of his 'love' for them, he graciously allowed his disciples to "die" for him but only symbolically.

Members could now die for the Imam without…. dying!!

The gates to the second heaven were exclusively opened for *Fidais!!*

The deal offered two heavens …. but not for the price of one!!

Only current members of Life could apply. Moreover, *Fidai* membership fee was higher than Life!!

Once again, wealthy saw the proposal as a picnic, a few within the middle class put a foot in the door whilst the lower class watched from a distance!!

Club Three: Noorani

A member of the *Fidai* had dedicated his entire life to the service of the Imam, had died for him, and had entered heaven twice.

Yet, the system insisted that this wasn't enough to earn the promise of further unknown and unexplained benefits in the afterlife.

This served as the cue for the next secretive *majalis*...Noorani.

The Prophet had declared four family members as his closest kin viz his daughter Fatima, Mawla Ali and grandsons Hasan and Husayn. Along with the prophet these family members are referred to as *ahl al- bayt* in the Islamic world.

K created his own version of *ahl e bayt* and named it...*Noorani family.*

A member of *Noorani majalis* would be deemed to be a member of Imam's biological family.

The paradox was undeniable!!

Biological relationship had just transcended the spiritual one!!

But K knew he could depend on the stupidity and willing blindness of his followers.

Yet again the wealthy paid a higher fee than Life and *Fidai* to belong to the most exclusive club….so far!!

Their financial sacrifices, they believed would open the gate to the third heaven!!

Once again, those who could afford the membership of three elite clubs, along with their corresponding and repetitive ongoing tributes, gained access.

The rest could seek consolation from the term…*my beloved spiritual children!!*

Club Four: One Fourth

By this point, the disciple had already committed to a lifetime of service to the Imam, had died for him as *Fidai,* and had been incorporated into the Imam's family through *Noorani.*

For these memberships, the disciples were already paying through their noses.

K realized that!!

So, the next and the last spiritual invention didn't require a membership fee!!

Rather, this time K went straight for the jugular!!

To enter One Fourth *majalis*, the spiritual fool would pay one fourth of his income instead of one eight as *dasond!!*

Appropriately he named it, One Fourth Majalis.

In summary K had invented and designed four secretive spiritual meetings to supplement nine public ones.

During six decades of his Imamate, money did not flow… it rained!!

Triple Dasond

Dasond literally means one tenth. Accordingly, in medieval times, the rate of *dasond* was set at one-tenth, or 10%. Over time, one of the Aga Khans saw an opportunity to impose an additional 2.5% charge. The new rate had been inflated to 12.5%.

Then the ever creative and unrelenting system had another Eureka moment!!

Triple *dasond!!*

The idea stemmed from the question of whether the *dasond* should be paid before or after government taxes were deducted from income.

The answer was obvious but not its methodology!!

To comprehend the idea, let's consider a family of four. A husband, wife, and two children. The husband is the sole breadwinner, earning $150,000 before taxes. The wife, a member of the One Fourth Majlis, receives $200 in weekly pocket money, while each child receives $50 weekly.

How much *dasond* would the family pay?

The first layer is 12.5% of the husband's pre-tax income of $150,000, which amounts to $18,750. The second layer is 25% of the wife's annual pocket money or $2600. Lastly, the children's 12.5% of $50 weekly each adds up to $650.

In total, the family would pay $22,000 *dasond* on a gross income of $150,000, which equates to a staggering 14.66% before tax.

Fifteen Billion Bottom Line

Dasond, membership fees, cash, jewelry *Mehmani* (gifts for the Imam), *Nandi* (food auction), *Awwal*

Sufro (auction of spiritual blessings), *Jamatkhana* Services Fund, an array of rituals and ceremonies, are just some of the revenue-generating methods at play in Jamatkhana.

But one wonders: how much did all this translate into dollar terms for K?

Unfortunately, due to the extreme secrecy surrounding the handling of money, no one knows. Most transactions are unreported cash deposited into K's Swiss bank accounts.

No one knows the exact amount—but with the right insight, a reasonable estimate isn't out of reach. As luck would have it, during my days as a devotee, I had a unique advantage of having served as a member of the Money Counting Committee at my local Jamatkhana.

In a team of five, we sorted, bundled, and recorded the cash in a register before depositing them in a vault. After the *Jamatkhana* closed, a mysterious figure would raid the vault and vanish into the night. That experience has provided me with an estimate of the contributions made by a typical devotee.

To arrive at an approximation, we need to assign values to two key variables: K's global following and the average tribute paid by each devotee.

Using formula AxB=C, where A represents the global following and B the average devotees' annual tribute, would provide the value of C …. the mysterious bottom line.

The challenge lies in determining the values of A and B. Fortunately, K himself has removed much of the guesswork regarding A…his following. During an interview, he did not respond when asked about leading fifteen million people, a tacit affirmation.

On the other hand, determining the annual tribute, value of B is complicated. However, my experience in the counting room may help.

For instance, in 2014, Sydney *jamaat's* average daily takings was $2,700. This amounted to approximately $1 million annually. Given a population of seven hundred, the average contribution per devotee was around AUD $1,400.

Hence, converted to US currency, the value of B was approx. US $1,000.00

Now, applying the A x B=C formula:

$$15,000,000 \times 1,000 = \$15,000,000,000$$

Therefore, it can be safely inferred that K's estimated annual spiritual income was staggering. $15 billion!

The figure may be rattling, but the true intrigue begins here.

White Collar Crime

A colossal amount was being generated from *Jamatkhanas* across the globe….in cash!!

Question arises: How is it transferred to K? Do the leaders dip dirty hands in the loot? Does K's share end up with a charity, as the Islamic mandate requires?

These questions have long occupied the minds of suspecting followers but asking them has always been taboo.

Then on 18 May 1987, the world got its first glimpse into the mystery of JK revenue!

Nizamuddin Alibhai, one of K's followers, boarded an American Airlines flight from Dallas-Fort Worth to London's Gatwick, carrying $1.1 million in a burgundy flight bag. He did not declare the stash, but an alert customs official uncovered it, nonetheless. Alibhai was arrested and taken to court.

During the proceedings, Prosecutor Stewart Robinson presented irrefutable evidence that Alibhai had unlawfully transferred $27.3 million out of the United States within a short time, thereby breaching legislation which mandates the declaration of transfers exceeding $10,000. Alibhai received a seven-year prison sentence in Dallas.

But who owned the money? Where did $27 million come from?

Two years later, the world woke up to reality.

On January 9, 1989, a Mercedes Benz bound for Canada from the US arrived at the Seattle Border for a routine customs check. The driver, Sadruddin Kabani, a devoted follower of K, declared, "Nothing to declare."

Yet, an alert customs officer discovered $1 million in cash hidden in the car's tire well. Kabani's arrest set off an investigation, revealing that the money had come from various *Jamaatkhanas* across the US, all destined for K's Swiss bank account.

Soon after, a sting operation led to the arrest of more disciples on money laundering charges. The Canadian Broadcasting Corporation (CBC) aired a documentary titled

God's Money, which told the entire story.

This moment was historic!

For the first time since becoming the forty-ninth Imam of the Nizari Ismailis, K was linked to white-collar crime but… not charged.

After all, it was not his fault that fools decided to stuff his bank account with money!!

Invincibility Formula

Harry Greenwall, in his book *Aga Khan III: Imam of the Ismailis*, writes:

"Among those people (murids), some are extremely rich and some are miserably poor. One may disregard for the moment the monies raised during His Highness's Diamond and Golden Jubilees and instead focus solely on the ordinary tributes. The extremely poor may contribute only copper annas, but the rich and very rich often donate large cheques sometimes as much as 1,000 pounds. Yet, if ten million people each give a yearly tribute of just five shillings, one can immediately see that this alone total fifty million shillings, which amounts to two and a half million pounds. If one then reasonably increases either the number of followers, bringing the figure closer to His Highness's

own estimate, or raises the yearly tribute, which is entirely justifiable the total becomes colossal, even without accounting for the income from other sources."

SMS was a mere British pensioner, yet during his lifetime, he became one of the wealthiest individuals of his time. K inherited the immense fortune upon SMS's passing, multiplying it many times over throughout his own reign.

Like SMS, K lived an unethical and immoral life in the pursuit of wealth. However, unlike his predecessor, K turned to white-collar crime.

After sixty-seven years of instigating crime, he remarkably evaded scrutiny, with only a few minor felony charges in East Africa cases from which he swiftly extricated himself.

But the question remains:

How did K deceive his followers and the global community, avoid scrutiny ...yet maintain his reputation as a humanitarian?

The answer lies in an unwritten and unprecedented three step Invincibility formula:

1) *Braindead disciples were to commit white collar crimes in the name of service to the Imam.*

2) *The Imam himself would hide behind the closed doors of his appointed institutions in Jamatkhana, and his development network Aga Khan Development Network (AKDN)*

3) *Imam would spend from the dirty money to buy accolades, citizenships, and titles with large donations to political parties around the world, thus creating an illusion of humanity.*

K was now invincible, thanks to a deadly mix of indoctrination, secrecy, propaganda, lies, and the ever-powerful influence of wealth.

Jamaatkhanas around the world would generate dirty money, which would be washed by in-house businesses, K's humanitarian network (AKDN), and tax havens, as we shall learn later in this chapter.

As if that were not enough, K had no qualms about lying.

During an interview with Portugal TV, the host asked,

"What do you think about the discussion in Islam that faith should be personal, i.e., Imams or mullahs should not direct it? It is something between you and your God."

K replied,

"Every individual is expected to use their intellect and knowledge to help understand their faith." That is the way we interpret faith. So, I do not see any conflict there."

He neglected to mention that he not only interferes in faith matters but operates an authoritarian cult collecting billions, all while pretending to be God.

In a separate interview, when questioned about his astronomical wealth, he commented,

"The fundamental principle for the wealthy is to use what they need to live with dignity. Share anything beyond that!

If one were to follow his example, one might need only a £250 million yacht, private jets, helicopters, private islands, elite stud farms and stables in Europe, a yacht club in Sardinia, prime real estate scattered across the globe, and a Swiss bank account brimming with unaccounted, unaudited cash to live with dignity!!

Chapter Four

Islamic Conscience

In 622 CE, the prophet migrated to Medina after enduring persecution in Mecca. The migrants had left behind their property, belongings, and livelihoods.

To facilitate their resettlement in Medina, the Prophet established a bond of brotherhood between each Medinan resident (Ansar) and the migrants (*Muhajir*). Regardless of their economic status, the *Ansars* supported and nurtured the *Muhajirun,* creating a network of solidarity and mutual assistance. Then *Zakat,* the obligatory charitable giving, became one of the five pillars of Islam.

Thus, the concept of Islamic Conscience was born.

AKDN

In modern times, K founded Aga Khan Development Network (AKDN), a mostly "not for profit" network of agencies albeit trading as mostly for profit, as we shall soon elaborate!

He named it after himself with the stated purpose of embodying Islamic Conscience.

However, a closer examination of AKDN suggests that its creation and objectives have served K's personal interests…funded by global taxpayers.

The Aga Khan Development Network (AKDN) is a global, non-denominational group of private agencies committed to improving the human condition. It operates through various agencies that provide essential services such as education, healthcare, and microfinance, while also promoting the revival and appreciation of art and architecture.

At the heart of AKDN's mission is the belief in pluralism as a core value, essential for fostering peace and progress.

According to its website, AKDN's efforts have led to significant milestones, including eight million outpatient visits across more than 700 health facilities, early childhood development programs for over 2.3 million preschool children, nearly one million students educated in over 200 schools and two universities, access to safe water for more than 770,000 people, the generation of 1.8 billion kWh of clean electricity, financial services for over 50 million people, the training of 40,000 community volunteers in disaster management, and the planting of more than 3.2 million trees.

AKDN's philosophy emphasizes teaching people to fish rather than giving them fish.

Despite popular perceptions, however, the network's mandate is to generate profit and function as a conduit of dirty money generated by *Jamatkhanas* around the world.

Aga Khan Health Services

Aga Khan Health Services is one such not-for-profit agencies of AKDN. It provides healthcare to eight million people annually. It operates twenty-two hospitals and over 700 healthcare centers in Afghanistan, India, Kenya, Kyrgyzstan, Pakistan, Syria, Tajikistan, Tanzania, and Uganda.

However, are the services provided on a charitable basis?

In 1967, President of Pakistan Zia ul Haq granted 68.5 acres of prime land in Karachi to K for the purpose of building a charitable hospital. The Aga Khan University Hospital (AKUH) was completed in 1985. Since then, governments have changed and so has K's commitment to charity.

It is an open secret that the hospital charges exorbitant fees for health services far beyond the reach of the middle class, let alone the poor.

In 2019, Karachi-based lawyer Dur Mohammad Shah filed a petition in the Sindh High Court, seeking clarity on AKUH's criteria for providing free healthcare to the needy. He stated that although the land was designated for charitable purposes, the healthcare costs at the hospital remained high for the poor.

The counsel representing AKUH confirmed that the land was allocated for charitable purposes and acknowledged that the government grants tax exemptions. However, they contended that charging patients did not negate the hospital's charitable nature. In defense of the exorbitant fees, they asked *how else could they run a state-of-the-art facility without charging?*

And so, the truth became known!

The true purpose of the project, after all, was not to serve the poor and the needy, but to create a state-of-the-art hospital designed to attract the wealthy.

It is worth noting that Muslims contribute *zakat* to AKUH, which qualifies for a tax deduction in Pakistan.

However, K does not allow any exemption from *dasond*, his religious tax, if his followers were to donate to AKUH!!

The Aga Khan Foundation

The Aga Khan Foundation (AKF) is a registered charity under the umbrella of AKDN. It is renowned as a leading global development organization dedicated to addressing the root causes of poverty.

It receives financial support from donations and grants provided by both public and private sectors globally. For instance, in 2013, Canada granted the foundation $41.9 million. Additionally, AKF raises funds from the global community through various initiatives, such as:

A. Donating directly to the foundation.

B. Joining the iHope community, which allows individuals to contribute collectively as a group.

C. Encouraging private sector employers to match donations dollar for dollar through the Employer Matching Gift Program.

D. Making a tribute donation in memory of a loved one via the Tribute Giving Page, shared with family and friends.

E. Transferring stock ownership to AKF.

F. Leaving a bequest to AKF in a will.

G. Nominating AKF as the beneficiary of a life insurance policy or retirement plan.

H. Rolling over retirement account distributions to benefit AKF.

Notably, K's followers actively participate in these initiatives, while also contributing billions in religious tributes.

However, these astronomical global inflows raise a question.

Why does the global public fund AKDN when it is a network of profitable development agencies disguised as not for profit?

The answer lies in secrecy and non-transparency!!

Non-Transparency

Although the AKDN website states that K personally contributes to his humanitarian network, it is not transparent on the issue.

A few years ago, I emailed AKDN for details on his contributions.

I was ignored!

(the email can be found in the appendix)

Then again according to a report, AKF held significant 'idle' property valued at $346.2 million in FY2013. Meanwhile, the Canada Revenue Agency found that The Aga Khan Foundation Canada (AKFC) had enough cash on hand to operate for up to eight years without raising a single penny.

Greg Thomson, Director of Charity Intelligence Canada, once remarked, quoting AKF Canada:

"Charities are not legally bound to disclose their audited financial statements to the public, but it is considered ethical to do so because they handle public dollars."

Property Scam

During my research over the years, I discovered another facet of AKF's operations. The foundation enabled K to profit from hundreds, if not thousands, of *Jamatkhana* properties worldwide.

When a new *Jamaatkhana* is needed, the local leaders must seek K's blessings which is usually granted.

This triggers a devotee stampede to contribute to the land and construction cost of the building. Thanks to indoctrination, they believe that helping build a *Jamaatkhana* would lead them to heaven.

The more they give, the greater their chances!

After the *Jamatkhana* is constructed, the title is gifted to K, who then sells the property to his own charity…the AKF!!

(The sale documents for the Hyderabad *Jamaatkhana* are included in the appendix)

The Aga Khan Fund for Economic Development

The Aga Khan Fund for Economic Development (AKFED) is the only official for-profit agency. According to its website, it is:

an international development agency dedicated to promoting entrepreneurship and building economically sound enterprises in the developing world.

However, on 25 August 2017, it became glaringly apparent that it also had a sinister function.

Following the arrest of Agakhan mules on money laundering charges in the late eighties, AKFED brought majority ownership in banks to facilitate the flow of dirty money from *Jamatkhanas*.

But in 2015, one of its banks was busted by US authorities!!

New York's Department of Financial Services (DFS) sought to impose a $630 million penalty on Habib Bank (HBL), majority-owned by AKFED. The penalty stemmed from HBL's repeated failure to comply with Anti-Money Laundering Laws and the Bank Secrecy Act.

The DFS report highlighted the bank's failure to screen and report transactions. These were linked to cybercriminals, arms manufacturers, a leader of a Pakistani terrorist organization, and Al Rajhi Bank of Saudi Arabia.

However, by agreeing to shut down its New York branch, HBL was able to reduce the penalty to $225 million.

Despite these revelations, it is striking that, as of this writing, *Jamatkhanas* worldwide, in collaboration with AKDN, continue to overlook the law.

Chapter Five

The Political Clout

Pakistan

They say money cannot buy everything.

True but it can buy public perception and politicians!!
In Pakistan, for example K hit the ground running.

Pakistan President Zia ul Haq inaugurating Agakhan University

SMS's crucial role in the creation of the nation has not been forgotten by its people. K, on his part, also commanded the same respect and reverence in the community. During his Imamate, he reinforced the illusion that the dynasty genuinely cared for the Muslim people. He invested heavily in Pakistan's infrastructure, founding schools and hospitals…albeit for selfish purposes.

Like SMS, K was a Muslim hero to the masses, but his influence in Pakistan ran much deeper.

Since migrating to Australia in 1984, I have visited Pakistan frequently, especially Karachi, where I met and married my wife. During one such visit in 2015, I met the director of a national television station, whom I initially believed was unaware of K's secret dealings.

As our conversation flowed, I began revealing what I thought would leave him in shock. To my surprise, after a brief pause, the director gestured for me to stop and calmly said,

'Salim, don't you think I know? But the day I run the story will be the last day for my TV station.'

I knew K was a respected figure in Pakistan, but I had no idea he was virtually untouchable. The director of the TV station subtly hinted that the media, at least, the traditional media, was under his control.

Furthermore, the Government was beholden to him through his financial influence.

As I would later discover, Pakistan symbolized K's reach across other third world countries in Asia and Africa. But did that mean he lacked influence in the west?

Canada

In his university days, K had been roommates with Pierre Trudeau at Harvard. Over time, Trudeau would go on to become Canada's Prime Minister, while K would become Aga Khan IV. Their enduring friendship played a pivotal role in helping relocate thousands of his followers during the 1972 Ugandan crisis as discussed earlier.

When I visited Toronto in late 2021, the Aga Khan Museum was high on my list of places to see. I was captivated by the striking architecture of the building, as well as the rich art and artifacts housed within.

What piqued my curiosity, however, was the donation board displayed prominently in the foyer. It proudly listed the names of donors who had given generously, some in the millions. What the board didn't reveal, hough, was the museuem received

=

substantial government grants and tax breaks. The property was valued at around $91 million, which should have attracted an annual property tax of $331,000.

Yet K never had to pay a cent!!

Although the Toronto Star had reported the preferential treatment as unfair to other museums, the Government turned a blind eye.

Then the Canada – Aga khan love affair took a darker turn.

In 2006, K established the Global Center for Pluralism (GCP) in Ottawa, aimed at promoting successful pluralistic societies worldwide. The Canadian government leased him a property that had once housed the Canadian War Museum for just $1 and granted him thirty million dollars to build the GCP.

But was the Canadian government's generosity well directed?

Would the people of Canada have granted millions to foster pluralism if they knew K himself ran an authoritarian cult behind closed doors?

The Ismaili Constitution freely available as a public document was ordained by K. Its authoritarian nature becomes apparent within the first few pages, where it grants K and his stooges sweeping powers, while making no mention of basic rights to his followers.

Furthermore, the system overseen by K rejects the basic human right of free speech and expression. If one dares to challenge him or his regime, they are ostracized. I am a living example and victim of K's authoritarianism, which I shall elaborate upon in the following pages.

In line with this totalistic tradition, in late 2023, the UK National Council threatened disciplinary action against disciples who chose to financially support their fellow disciples rather than giving to *Mukhi*, K's representative.

(the transcript is in the appendix)

As for whether Canadian taxpayer money has made the world any more pluralistic, remains open to debate. Meanwhile, the GCP's impressive building in Ottawa continues to host lectures, award ceremonies, and produce reports on the human condition.

But then, the Canadian politicians kicked their people in the gut when K was allowed to lease the GCP building back to the government for a hefty rent!!

K would now receive income from the very gift that Canadian public had given him!!

Agakhan Affair

The Canadian media had long suspected K's sinister operations. Their suspicions were confirmed in December 2016 when PM Trudeau accepted K's invitation to his private residence in Bell Cay, Bahamas.

K with Canadian PM Trudeau

Along with the invitation, the Prime Minister accepted gifts and a flight in K's private helicopter. This conduct violated the Federal Conflict of Interest Act. In the Ethics Commission hearing, the accused PM claimed they were family friends, and the trip was personal.

However, Commissioner Mary Dawson rejected his argument, stating:

"There were no private interactions between Mr. Trudeau and the Aga Khan until Mr. Trudeau became Leader of the Liberal Party of Canada. This led me to conclude that their relationship cannot be described as one of friends for the Act."

The tax breaks for the Aga Khan Museum, the GCP scandal, Agakhan Affair, the ongoing millions in grants to Aga Khan Foundation Canada, and the money laundering activities linked to the *Jamatkhana* have cost Canadian taxpayers hundreds of millions, if not billions over six decades of K's reign.

Despite this, both sides of Parliament have, not only turned a blind eye but awarded an honorary Canadian citizenship to K!!

France

SMS had spent much of his life on the French Riviera, unaware that France would one day become the future headquarters of the *Nizari Imamate.*

Upon assuming the office of the Imamate in 1957, K developed deep roots in France. He established his residence and Imamate Secretariat, in Aiglemont, a three-hour drive from Paris.

For the next five decades, it would not only be his home but also the headquarters of his global spiritual empire and humanitarian network, the AKDN.

However, as his career neared its twilight, dark clouds gathered on the horizon. The looming storm would soon uproot him and his entire system from France.

In 2007, it all began with the downfall of French President Sarkozy. He had invoked 'special' powers to relieve K of direct taxes, stamp duty, and wealth tax, citing his status as a descendant of Prophet Muhammad and his tireless efforts to improve the human condition.

K with Sarkozy and Karzai

The French public and media were puzzled as to why a descendant of an Islamic Prophet (if indeed he was) was prioritized over the needs of the French people and its humanitarian efforts.

But the broader question was:

Why did multi-billionaires like K need tax breaks?

Growing Frech curiosity eventually led to an official investigation into Sarkozy's conduct in 2012, which culminated in his conviction for 'active corruption'

He was sent to prison!

This was a turning point in K's life.

His friend was in jail, and he had fallen out of favor with the incoming Socialist Party. It swiftly revoked the preferential tax treatment extended to K. Consequently, the Sarkozy affair altered K's "humanitarian" image in France.

After spending five decades in France, it was time to move on!!

But where would he nest?

Wherever it was, he needed tax exemptions, but more importantly… legal immunity. Thanks to the power of the internet, his underground dealings and global scams were beginning to surface.

Canada seemed like the perfect choice. After all, K had enjoyed close ties with both major political parties, the Liberals and the Conservatives. However, Canada's open democracy didn't allow for tax exemptions or legal immunity.

It wasn't long before K found the perfect refuge!

Portugal: The Haven

At the turn of the millennium, the world's outlook was bleak. The Global Financial Crisis (GFC) caused many economies across the globe to shrink, and in some cases, to collapse. One of the most vulnerable countries was Portugal, deemed a flawed democracy by the Economist Intelligence Unit.

From 2011 to 2013, Portugal's economy contracted for three consecutive years, and unemployment soared, triggering a cascade of domestic problems.

Fortunately, Portugal was a member of the European Union, which came to its aid with a bailout of seventy-eight billion Euros. While this financial support kept Portugal afloat, the country remained in deep trouble. Every bit of help was crucial to reaching safer ground.

Meanwhile K, the multi billionaire, had been seeking a haven!!

Portugal eagerly embraced his fifteen-billion-dollar black economy. The country extended K a generous offer: diplomatic status, the ability to transfer global assets, tax exemptions, and most crucially legal immunity.

Welcoming K to Portugal, President De Souza declared:

"What brings us together is a joint commitment to defend and uphold the principles and values that honor the importance of ethical standards in human life, the pluralism of societies, and respect for human dignity."

K with President De Sousa

On 8 October 2020, a diplomatic agreement was signed between the *Ismaili Imamate* and the Portuguese Republic.

That same year, K purchased the Palacete Henrique Mendonca in Lisbon, which became both the global headquarters of the *Ismaili Imamate* and his personal residence.

The mission had been accomplished: he had found a Haven.

But unexpectedly... he vanished into it!!

Chapter Six

The Common Man

As discussed in the introduction of this work, in 2014 I uncovered the dark underbelly of Agakhanism. Upon renouncing my faith, I embarked on a journey of researching, learning and gathering evidence. Over this seven-year period of discovery, I found that the system not only exploited blindfolded followers but also manipulated the global community and desecrated the Holy Qur'an.

I wanted K and his system to either discontinue or reform their system to discontinue the abuse.

In my naivety, I did not understand, fulfilling my wish would mean dismantling a multi-billion-dollar enterprise!!

I decided to open a dialogue with the then-President of the Australia and New Zealand Council, Karim Sumar.

We met at a local coffee shop, where I explained that I had found evidence of moral, ethical, and legal wrongdoing within the system. I raised concerns about Islamic blasphemy and the financial abuse of the *jamaat* in the name of humanity and spirituality. I suggested that the system take immediate steps to rectify these issues, warning that, should they fail to do so, I would be forced to go public.

As expected, Sumar was in denial!!

Consumed by the typical Agakhani arrogance, he slyly remarked,

"I suggest you concentrate on Cambodia"

Back then, I had volunteered to work for a humanitarian cause in the Far East.

Yes, his arrogance was evident, but it was not unreasonable. Many rebels before me, particularly in British India had raised their voices, only to be silenced by the system's brutal practice of excommunication and ostracism.

A few had gone missing!!

But blinded by arrogance, Sumar overlooked the fact that he was dealing with a rebel in a new age of internet, which had potential to cause irreversible reputational damage.

In any case, the meeting ended in disagreement. I was ignored and possibly discounted as a madman.

By this time, it had dawned upon me that my odds of being heard were almost zero.

But for some unknown reason I chose to blow the whistle!!

After the arrow had left the bow, I realized that irrespective of my success or failure, I would be judged, potentially abused, and even killed.

But I took consolation in the fact that I was no ordinary David, taking on a Goliath. I was armed with internet, an unprecedented and a powerful tool…. It's reach global, its speed lightning and its force devastating!!

In some corner of my heart, I knew if I used its power to spread the truth, it would likely discredit K, undermine his clout, and threaten his veneration and perhaps even his bottom line.

Would that not be enough to bring K to the table? I thought.

The Rebel

My YouTube channel, Diary of a Common Man, debuted on 21 January 2021. I had now officially become both a rebel and a whistleblower. My message was simple:

Give to the Poor, Not Agacon!

The first episode sent shockwaves through K's global community.

After all, someone had dared to speak the truth in public, an incredibly rare occurrence in the system's history.

As expected, my voice shook K's followers and his leadership…globally.

Simultaneously, it also shook someone's grave!!

Ghost of SMS, Sultan Mohammad Shah, Aga Khan III, the forty eighth Nizari Imam rose from the dead to haunt me!!

Ostracism was first practiced by the ancient Greeks to neutralize potential rebellions. It involved shunning and shaming the victim, condemning them to ten years of isolation.

SMS in his era, took this punitive concept and twisted it into something far more inhumane. The victim would be totally boycotted and ostracized.

Entry into *Jamatkhana* would be prohibited, his *jamaat*, family and friends would abandon him, he would be banned from commercial activities, denied the essential transactions necessary for survival, and along with his family, he would carry the stigma of rebellion for life.

Ultimately in death, he would be denied the rites of burial!!

The consequences were so extreme that the *jamaat* didn't just conform; they proactively boycotted anyone who didn't.

Over time, this inhuman practice became ingrained in their psyche and the barbaric legacy of SMS was passed down to future generations.

When I rebelled in the new millennium, I wasn't sure whether SMS's legacy had survived!

Thus, I had reason to be optimistic.

After all, are we not more educated than in SMS's time? Do we not live in a more civilized society that upholds basic human rights, including freedom of speech and expression? Do we not live in an information age?

But to my utter surprise, I was proven wrong by my small jamaat in Sydney.

They demonstrated that they were degree holders but not educated, they demonstrated that they belonged to an uncivilized society that rejects basic human rights, including freedom of speech and expression, and they revealed that, despite their modern outlook, their thinking remained primitive.

SMS legacy was not only living in the 21st century, but it was thriving!!

I was ostracized!!

Evil Cult

When my first video aired, my *jamaat* wasn't instructed by K or the leadership to turn against me. It happened on its own.

My circle of friends with whom I had spent decades together, distanced themselves, my clients within the *jamaat* withdrew their business, triggering a personal financial collapse. I received cold looks on the street, was spat at, and faced vicious cyber backlash.

But there was more to come!!

My children abandoned me, which separated me from my grandchildren, one of whom I still haven't seen since his birth three years ago.

And then came the final blow for which I was utterly unprepared!!

My forty-year marriage collapsed. The mother of my two children, my soul mate, my best friend, and my wife without whom I couldn't imagine life, separated from me. Me and along with my distressed mother appealed for a dialogue and counselling but to no avail.

Without a doubt, the separation from my wife traumatized me like no other pain that I have endured in my existence over sixty-six years.

Yet, somehow, I survived the schemes of the evil cult emotionally, psychologically, socially, and financially.

Not only did I survive, but I also found strength in solitude to advance my struggle. This strength was a direct result of the priceless moral support of thousands around the world who backed my campaign, the donors, volunteers, my brother, and, above all, unconditional and uncorrupted love of my mother.

At the time of writing, I am alone but not lonely. I have three companions: my mission to raise awareness, my spiritual journey, and my most loyal and loving dog Bella.

First Ray of Light

I had watered the seed of my campaign with my own blood, so it was no surprise that the first fruits of my sacrifices began to show within months of my first appearance on air.

Consistent reports from supporters inside the *Jamatkhanas* around the globe indicated that *Awwal Sufro* bids were falling.

This was significant news!

***Awwal Sufro* is the congregational auction of, believe it or not, spiritual blessings!!**

Yes, spiritual blessings are auctioned to the highest bidder. These public bids are the only clear indicator of the system's bottom line. All other financial transactions occur secretly, between the disciple and *Mukhi*.

Global supporters consistently reported an average decline of 60% in winning bids. This drop meant that not only was I being heard by the global *jamaat,* but my message *Give to the poor, not Agacon* had struck a chord.

Traditionally, the system adopts an Ostrich policy in response to challenges, i.e. burying their heads in the sand, waiting for the storm to pass.

But this time, the crisis was unprecedented—spiritual revenue was plummeting like never before. A solution had to be found.

They had no choice but to abandon the Ostrich policy!!

Intimidation

To begin with, Karim Sumar, the President of the Council, who had ridiculed me only a few months prior, sent me a cease-and-desist letter, a legal threat.

In the letter, he accused me of spreading false information and disturbing the peace of the *jamaat*. Furthermore, he demanded that I remove the posted material from social media and refrain from further posts.

In response, I counter challenged him to prove his accusations and vehemently refused to take down any material from social media.

Sumar had fallen flat on his face and with him, the credibility of the mighty Aga Khan!!

True to form, he dug his head in the sand once more. Three months passed; the problem remained unresolved, the revenue continued to bleed!!

Bribe

In May 2021, I received a call from London. The caller introduced himself as Alfie, an "ardent fan." He explained that he had been born into the Aga Khan faith but left it when he came of age. His mother, still a disciple, remained unaware of his disaffiliation, so he wished to stay anonymous for fear of harassment from the system.

Professionally, he worked as a bank employee, specializing in money laundering investigations. To me, he was just what the doctor ordered, an angel who had descended from the skies!!

Over the next few months, we spent time preparing and strategizing to infiltrate the scam. But one day, Alfie informed me that he could no longer assist. He "assessed" that an offer was forthcoming, and he named it!!

$25 million!!

He feared I would accept it, and his investment of time and energy would go to waste. In response, I reassured him that I would not accept the bribe if it was to eventuate.

That was the last time I heard from him!!

Later that month, another call came, once again from London. This time, Karim, a fan and a lawyer, claimed he could help with "nailing" K legally.

However, three weeks into our partnership he began imagining that I would be "bought out" .... again for $25 million. When I assured him that I was not for sale, he disappeared like dew evaporating in the afternoon sun.

Assassination?

Local leadership's verbal and legal threats had backfired. Then two attempts to bribe me from top leadership had also failed. If anything, they had made my resolve stronger. The cult had one more card up their sleeve.

Silence me for good!!

K's followers, at least in the present times are a meek lot!! They offer a stark contrast to their forefathers who had killed and got killed during Aga Khan I and Aga Khan III's times as discussed in previous chapters. But then, for almost a century, the system had not faced a challenge such as this.

A challenge powered by the Almighty Internet!!

It was an extraordinary problem, and the system was fast running out of options.

If I had been rebelling in a pre-internet era, my assassination would surely have solved the problem, as was the case in Karachi a few decades earlier.

Unfortunately, for the system, in the internet age, my assassination would only compound the problem rather than solve it. They could have me killed but not the speed of information nor my digital footprint!!

Furthermore, the act of violence would convince the global public and the *Jamaat* that Agakhanism is not only a fraudulent system, but also a criminal mafia.

After such revelations, would the global public donate to Aga Khan institutions as they do now? Would the system's spiritual scam survive?

It is no wonder that I survived. But my survival was a threat to the system. Having exhausted all options, the system eventually deployed its most deadly weapon!!

Carter Ruck: K's Lawyer

Carter Ruck is one of the most famous law firms in English legal history. Bureau of Investigative Journalism once remarked:

Those who receive letters from firms like Carter-Ruck often back down not because they have a weak case, but because the cost of fighting a claim can become crippling.

Yet another lawyer said:

They probably are the most feared claimant firm in the UK,

In 2021, several months since my first episode, I received a cease-and-desist letter from the feared Carter Ruck!!

Their client was the National Council for Australia and New Zealand but it was glaringly apparent that it was K's stooges in Europe acting on his behalf.

When I received the email, I wondered…*Why would Carter Ruck, the legal giant, try to intimidate a common man?*

After all, the National Council for Australia and New Zealand had used a local storefront lawyer just a few months earlier to send a similar threat.

Whilst K's letter accused me of spreading false information, it was clearly apparent that the system was concerned about my revelations of s*hirk* in *Jamatkhanas* and how it could mean bad news for his followers in Islamic countries.

The letter reads:

You are hereby notified that the publication of these videos particularly regarding the Blasphemy Allegation poses a significant risk of violence against Ismaili Muslims, both within the countries involved and beyond.

As you are undoubtedly aware, extremist elements within certain Muslim communities have repeatedly engaged in acts of intimidation and deadly violence against other Muslims, particularly Shia Muslims, globally. Ismaili Muslims have been among the victims of these attacks. Large communities of Ismaili Muslims currently reside in countries like Pakistan and Afghanistan, where allegations of blasphemy often provoke intense and violent reactions. Historically, Ismailis have faced violent and deadly assaults from such extremists.

You are aware of this history, as evidenced in the videos themselves, where you reference an incident from five years ago in which 45 Ismailis were murdered on a bus in Pakistan. You have acknowledged the importance of considering such events in determining whether to publish these videos in Urdu. Nonetheless, you have opted to move forward with publishing the videos in Urdu.

Our client has made multiple attempts to engage you on this issue and reiterates its request for the removal of the videos and a cessation of further publications that may incite harm. Should any harm come to Ismaili Muslims because of your videos, you will be held responsible.

With the hiring of Carter Ruck, K or his stooges may have been attempting another intimidation, only this time with a show of muscles.

But once again, in their arrogance, they made a costly and almost fatal blunder!!

Historic Blunder

It was obvious that they had not learnt from history. Only a few months earlier, President Karim Sumar's arrogance had triggered a revenue decline.

Besides, the recent threat from Carter Ruck was a testimony to the fact that they had not considered the consequences of a counter challenge from me… which soon arrived!!

My lawyers, Harish Jagtiani & Associates, responded to Carter Ruck.

The response made it clear to K or his stooges that I stood by the contents of my videos as they were based on verifiable truths.

Concerning the risk of potential backlash from the Muslim *ummah,* I reminded K that I was merely exposing his self-proclaimed divinity.

Furthermore, I also expressed my surprise that, despite the direct content aimed at him, K chose not to confront me. Instead, he hid behind the National Council for Australia and New Zealand, avoiding any personal challenge.

(The legal exchange can be found in the appendix)

Not only was Carter Ruck letter an attempt to intimidate me, but it was also a public testament to the system's deep concern over declining spiritual revenue and the possibility of a Muslim backlash.... potentially violent!!

The global jamaat watched in horror, as their *Mushkil Kusha*, the destroyer of difficulties, their Imam Shah Karim al Husayni, Agakhan IV was unable to restrain a common man!!

The Carter Ruck incident had significant consequences. K's divinity, infallibility, and invincibility had been shattered!!

The K and or the stooges had shot themselves in the foot. Limping in pain they retreated to the safety of their hiding hole!!

Soon I received messages from across the globe that the revenue was now falling at a much faster pace!!

From that point onward, it was all downhill for K....
the revenue, reverence, and his health.

Death and Succession

They say that animals have a way of dying that
differs from humans. Unless killed by another animal or
some external force, when their time comes, they retreat to a
secluded spot to pass away in peace.

Since moving to Lisbon Palace in 2015, seventy-
nine-year-old K, Aga Khan IV, withdrew from public life.
Later, the system released an image of a man... old, frail,
and ill. It was apparent that the stooges were running the
franchise on his behalf.

In any case, four years passed, the global
community, particularly his followers wondered if K was
dead or alive?

Nizari Ismaili history was repeating itself.

Imam Mustansir Billah, the last Fatimid Caliph was
the eighteenth Ismaili Imam. Towards the end of his life, he
was old, weak and frail. From his deathbed he had been
watching the dark clouds of disaster closing in on his empire.

Natural disasters, political turmoil, and his own impotence had loosened Ismaili grip on the *Fatimid Caliphate*.

Upon his death, the Caliphate had been lost to *Abbasids*. With his successor, *Nizar,* killed, and his descendants vanishing into the depths of obscurity, the *Ismaili Imamate* had been fractured.

K faced a similar set of circumstances on his deathbed in the Lisbon palace. He was old, frail and anticipated the angel of death to put an end to his immoral and unethical life. Most importantly, he saw dark clouds of doom gather over *Nizari Ismaili Imamate*.

Russia had banned his development network, Tajikistan revoked the licenses of his humanitarian agencies, while China raised a red flag on his suspicious activities in the region. International media was waking up to his corrupt regime.

Although the clubbers, at least at the time of writing kept the buzz alive in the *Jamatkhanas*, the youth, once responsible for sustaining the system, were exiting in droves; revenue was plummeting, long shadow of the law was lurking and the internet had flung the doors of the *Jamatkhana* wide open, thus exposing the immoral, unethical, illegal and anti-Islamic activities.

Under these circumstances, on 4th February 2025, the stooges announced K's death in Lisbon. He was buried in Aswan, the family burial ground.

His elder son, Rahim became Aga Khan V and 50th Nizari Ismaili Imam.

The Sinking Ship

In 1912, the Titanic, the unsinkable ship, had sunk. Coincidentally, around that same time, SMS built Agakhanism: his own Titanic.

At the time, it was unsinkable, but during the twilight of K's career, it struck an iceberg known as the internet.

It was no longer a matter of if… but when!!

Only time will tell if Jesus (new Imam's nick name) will attempt to fix the gash on the side of his Titanic or will he abandon the sinking ship.

Irrespective of his choice, it is glaringly apparent that Agakhan Titanic is doomed!!

Bibliography

Administration on Sindh	Sir William Napier
Aly	Leonard Slater
Brainwashing	Kathleen Taylor
For Arguments Sake	Tom Stafford
His Highness the Agakhan	Harry J Greenwall
Ibrat-afza	Agakhan I
Ismaili Literature	W. Ivanow
Ismailies: Their History and Doctrines	Dr Farhad Daftary
Kalam e Mowla Farmans	Agakhan III
Mein Kampf	Adolf Hitler
Memoirs of Agakhan	Agakhan III
No Bed of Roses	Joanne Fontaine
Shia of India	John N Hollister
The Agakhans	Willi Frischauer
The Agakhans	Mihir Bose
The Assasins of Alamut	Anthony Campbell
The Ismaili Constitution	Agakhan IV
The Paris Conference	Eqbal Rupani
Throne of Gold	Anne Edwards
Travels of Marco Polo	Marco Polo

Archives

Times of India

Poonah Observer

Aligarh Muslim University

London Sunday Pictorial

Life Magazine

India Office Library London

Letters of Agakhan III

Letters of Sir Arthur Hertzel

Memo of Sir Gilbert Laithwaite

Publication

Harvard University (Dr. Anthony Komaroff)

Thesis

Across the threshold of Modernity (Marco van Grondelle)

Documentary

CBC (God's Money)

Besides the above resources, I have referred to multiple websites including Ismaili.net.

Genealogy of Ismaili Nizari Imams (Agakhan Version)

Aly

Husayn

Zainil 'Abideen.

Muhammadinil Baqir

Ja'faris Sadiq

Ismail

Muhmmad bin Ismail,

Wafi Ahmed

Taqi Muhammad.

Raziyiddeen Abdillah

Muhammadinil Mahdi,

Qaim

Mansoor

Mu'izz

Aziz

Hakim bi Amrillah

Zahir

Mustansiribillah I

Nizar I

Hadi

Muhtadi

Qahir

Ala Zikrihis-Salaam

A'ala Muhammad

Jalaliddeen Hasan

Ala-iddeen Muhammad

Rukniddeen Khairi Shah

Shamsiddeen Muhammad

Qasim Shah

Islam Shah

Muhammad bin Islam Shah

Mustansiri-billah II

Abdis-Salaam

Ghareeb Meerza

Abizzar Aly

Murad Meerza

Zulfiqar Aly

Nooridden Aly

Khalilillahi Aly

Nizar II

Sayyid Aly

Hasan Aly

Qasim Aly

Abul Hasan Aly

Khalilillahi Aly

Shah Hasan Aly

Shah 'Aly Shah

Sultan Muhammad Shah

Karim al-Husayni

Rahim al Husayni

Translation

Ahl e Bayt: Members of the Prophet's House.

Alakh Niranjan: Beyond Comprehension

Alid: Descendant of Imam Ali

Amr: Divine command

Ansar: Helper

Avatara: Descent or incarnation

Ayat: Verse

Barbhaya: Twelve brothers

Baya'h: Oath of Allegiance

Brahma: Hindu God of Creation

Chhanta; Sprinkling of holy water

Dai: Missionary

Darbar: Audience given to the subjects by a king

Das avatar: Ten incarnation of a Hindu God

Dasond: 12.5% Agakhan Religious tax

Dawa: Invitation to an ideology

Dawr e Satr: Period of Concealment

Dawr e Kashf: Period of Manifestation

Deedar; A public audience

Dhikr: Chanting

Fana fila: To become one in God

Farman: Religious edict

Fidai: Someone willing to die for someone or something.

Fidayeen: Plural of Fidai

Garbi: Folk song of India

Gata: Congregation

Ginan: Nizari Devotional hymn

Hai Zinda; Ever prest

Hajj: Annual Holy pilgrimage to Mecca

Hashishin: User of Cannabis

Hujja: Authority

Imam: An Islamic spiritual leader

Imsak: Control over self

Ismailis: A Sect of Shia Islam

Istighfar; Islamic confession of sins

Ithna'Ashariyya: A sect of Shia Islam

Jallad: Executioner

Jamaat: Congregaion

Jamaatkana: A place of Agakhan worship

JK: Jamaatkana, a place of Agakhan worship

Juro: Food offering

K; Agakhan IV

Kaaba: Holy Islamic Shrine in Mecca

Kalki: Awaited incarnation of a Hindu God

Kamaria: Mukhi's assistant

Kayam paya; Something achieved for good

Khanaqah: Sufi place of worship

Khatam ul Anbiya: The seal of prophets

Khawaja: Saint

Khoja: A follower of Agakhan

Khojki: An Indian Script

Khudawind; Master

Mahadan: Day of Judgement

Majalis: A religious meeting

Masum: Infallible

Mazhar: Manifestion

Mehmani: Gifts presented to a guest

Meraj: The prophet's miraculous journey to heaven

Mohajir: Emigrant

Mowla: Master

Muhkamat: Easy to comprehend

Mukhi: Spiritual representative of Agakhan

Mukhiani: Mukhi's wife

Murid: Follower

Murshid: Master

Mushkil Kusha: Destroyer of difficulties

Muslim: Follower of the religion of Islam

Muta'h: A fixed term marriage contract

Mutashabihat: Difficult to comprehend

Naklanki: Someone without a blemish

Nizaris: Spiritual followers of Agakhan

Paat: A wooden table

Pir: Saint

Qasida: Central Asian devotional hymn

Quran: The Islamic holy scripture

Rashidun Caliph: Rightly Guided Caliph

Roshni; Light

Ruhani; Spiritual

Salaat: Muslim prayer

Salwat: An Islamic supplication

Satguru: True Master

Sawaab: Spiritual reward

Sawm: Fasting

Shahada: Declaration of Faith

Shia Imam: Imam Ali and his progeny

Shirk: Associating partners with God

Shura: Council

SMS: Agakhan III Sultan Mohammad Shah

Sunna: Legacy

Sura: Verse

Tafseer: Interpretation

Taqiyya: Hiding one's faith

Tassawwuf: Sufism

Ummah: The Islamic community

Vishnu: Hindu God of Destruction

Vizier: Prime Minister

Waez; Religious discourse

Waezeen; Missionary

Yaum e ali: Shia Imam Ali's birth anniversary

Yaum e Qiyama: Day of Resurrection

Zakat: Muslim Religious Tax

Ziyarat: Pilgrimage to the place of worship

Appendix 1

The Paris Conference Report

REPORT OF THE
ISMAILIA ASSOCIATION CONFERENCE
PARIS - APRIL, 1975

CONTENTS

		Page No.
PREFACE		
LIST OF DELEGATES		1 - 4
SUBJECTS:		
1.	REVIEW OF FUNDAMENTAL CONCEPTS AND BELIEFS:	
	1.1 Fundamental Concepts and Beliefs	5 - 7
	1.2 Spiritual Aspects of Ismailism	8 - 9
2.	RELIGIOUS RITES, RITUALS AND CEREMONIES	10 - 13
3.	RESEARCH ACTIVITIES:	
	3.1 The Institute of Ismaili Studies	14 - 19
	3.2 Ismaili History	20
	3.3 Nooran Mubeen	21 - 22
4.	RELIGIOUS EDUCATION:	
	4.1 General	23 - 24
	4.2 Programme of preparing an overall plan	24 - 27
	4.3 Progress Reports	27

(ii)

Page No.

5. MISSION WORK AND MISSIONARIES:

    5.1   General   28 - 29

    5.2   Training Programme for Waezeen/
          Religion Teachers   30 - 32

    5.3   Functions of Ismailia Associations
          in Waezeen activities   32 - 36

          Expenditure Chart   37 - 38

6. PUBLICATIONS:

    6.1   Publications by Ismaili individuals
          and institutions   39 - 40

    6.2   Printing of Firmans   41 - 45

    6.3   Printing of Ginans   46 - 47

7. ADMISSION INTO THE ISMAILI FAITH   48 - 49

8. ROLE AND STATUS OF ISMAILIA ASSOCIATIONS:

    8.1   Nomenclature   50

    8.2   Extension of Participation   50

    8.3   Functions of the Ismailia Associations   50 - 51

    8.4   Review Meetings and Conferences   51 - 53

    8.5   Co-ordinating Office   53

RESPONSIBILITY CHART   54 - 59

P R E F A C E

This report incorporates the resolutions of the Ismailia Association Conference which took place in Paris between the 1st and 5th April, 1975, both days inclusive. Mowlana Hazar Imam Shah Karim Al-Hussaini chaired the Conference, and all the resolutions contained herein are based on guidance received from, and as finally approved by, Mowlana Hazar Imam.

The Conference was convened, pursuant to Mowlana Hazar Imam's directive, by Count Sir Eboo Pirbhai, President of H.H. The Aga Khan Supreme Council for Europe, Canada and the U.S.A., and of H.H. The Aga Khan Supreme Council for Africa. Prior to it, two preparatory Conferences were also held, both under the Chairmanship of Count Sir Eboo, during which the preliminary work for the Paris Conference was undertaken. The first preparatory Conference took place in Nairobi in February, 1974, and the second in Paris in March, 1975. This report is, therefore, to be read in the context of the report of the 1974 Nairobi Conference.

The list of delegates who attended the 1975 Paris Conference is given overleaf.

EQBAL RUPANI
Co-ordinator
Ismailia Association Central
Co-ordinating Office

NAIROBI: 5th May, 1975

I. VIEW OF FUNDAMI:';1-:TAf;- GO;-;'CE;?TS AND DF.I.IEFS

1.1 Pund:iment:iJ' Cor.cepts and Elelie!s

The pre•Ccn!ercnce meetiJ\e; in :?a.rl.s revtewt:d the rccomrocndatione of the Nairobi Confe:rence, whi h *were* U..a.t. the following :.reas in Illlamic anc Ism.1ili religious thought and phU01,ophy should .rt<ce vo spei:i l emphasi.6 in. aU edilcilliorw and :re.i;e::u-cb prog,limmcs:

> (i) The cuncept of Goe
>
> (ii) **11he** co11cepts of Naouw:a :wd Imi\mah
>
> (111) Thi! concept of iv'..a11
>
> (iv) '!'he concept. oJ Religion

It wa,; AGREED lha the .i;cope or er.qu!fy under lhP. above **ue11.e** flhOUld o..160 cover the expo&itlOh of concepta lJUCh ae T,mzE:el 11.nd Qi •a.m:i.t,

The prc-Contere,11.:.,:meetin&--11>Oil:ic\l d a il:lp!!r tabl u lly the :&mail1a Ati.sod:dion !or P 1£t..n, e71titlE!d "FundamentA.! Bellc!1:1 u! 1.J;maill&",

Ou the irubJf!Ct of the key .reai:: rl!f<!r:ed lo above, Mowl:iru,, lia:i.ar J1n11.1T.1 directed that an uea dP.a.lIng with tJ111 relationship bellveen M:acter nd Spl.ril **be** Rrlci d to tlie four areas ii.lre:11dy• 1dentl.1ieo:. The Coufe;re1,t:c ll:creui,oo n.E$i0LVED that tt.e follo"':'ln shou:d !or,:.i the b:;.i;:s ol the ,laul:l.I'B approach tow:uci.s TP.l!gious edi:c:>.tl<.m and :-e1:;1::uch p.:-ogramm s:

ro   <u>The concept o.f God:</u>

The :.bsolute L.mecedar.te of God to be emphaslBed.,
and the ismaiH belief 1.i God to be e:xpoonded in
- asaociaUon w1t.h tlk: general 6t"e86 on t!ie transcedance
of God 1n the K.?;a;;, as t:xen;, lifi.ed iy   in the
lluat-u-llthlas.

<u>The concl!!)ts of :t2'c:n.r.:.li ti. .l!lar.:ah:</u>

These concepts tc t.; u7lahe<i ar.d ui!derciood 1ll llie
gena.:u perspective of Gcd'.; comm1micat:on to man.
The limm to ba ϵ   2.5 th.a '.L;uilil" of God,
a.'ld the rsW:io:ishlp bc--tween God a.'ll: tlie Irr.am to be
rslaled to var}'il:: levelll 0: !r.spi.-Aiiou and cfli"ilcm1nica-
t1011 from God to f.lall.

(111j   <u>The-concept of 11-ian:</u>

The:spiritual side of man, which 1s the mainBhy of
lslamic and l6mal!i to epti;Jllli of sel.fbooo,, to be
emphasi&ed and explaJJ.ed, d the L-ifllience of
Western idc-ologies wbe,eby the lila1Eri:;Jist.Jt conceptlon
of m:m Is likely iO berome izcrea.s y prsdommant
to -be talen acCOUiil. of,

(lv)   <u>The concept of Re!1¥1rm:</u>

This to be expWnec! L1 !me with tla: .hfo:nic
und r6tandir.g of re! ..oc as a whole vay of We.
In   th:i history of Jsla.:;J 4lld JsiGariam,

Appendix 2

Hyderabad Jamatkhana Sale

Dated this 26th day of March 1979.

HIS ROYAL HIGHNESS SHAH KARIM AL-HUSEINI

AGA KHAN

TO

FONDATION AGA KHAN

→ KIATEN
By NIZARDINSHAH THARMANI
AND RUKNUDINDSHAH HEMANI
IK DOCUMENT NO APD-3(6 TO
HOSTEL   No APD-5(6 TO

PR. 450

Presented at the office of the
Sub-Registrar of 'Bombay'
between the hours of 11 A.M.
and 12 No., on the 30th March
79

His Royal Highness
Shah Karim Al-Hussaini Aga Khan
by the hand of his Constituted Attorney.

Ameerali S. Rahimtoola

Sub-Registrar of Bombay
exercising all the powers of
a Registrar except that of
whether appeals.

A65-3
①

	Rs.	P.
Registration	1800	00
Copying		
(Rule 1)		60
End. Fee	1	00
Filing	1	00
Comparing		
(Rule 20)	1	00
Extra c/o 30	25	50
1 copy Rs.67	2	50
5 Memo	2	00
Postage		00
Total Rs.	**1846**	**00**

Sub. Registrar
of Bombay

THIS INDENTURE made at Bombay this 26th
day of March 1979 BETWEEN His Royal Highness
Shah Karim Al-Hussini Aga Khan of Switzerland, the 49th Imam
of the Shia Imami Ismaili Muslims, by the hand of his duly
constituted attorney Ameerali Sulaman Rahimtoola of Bombay
Indian Inhabitant having his office at Bhupen Chambers, Dalal

CERTIFIED
COPY

JOINT SUB-REGISTRAR-11
R.O. HYDERABAD

Page | 363

पा.ब. २

Street, Bombay 400-023 hereinafter called "the Vendor" (which expression shall unless repugnant to the context or meaning thereof mean and include him and his successor or successors in title) of the One Part and Fondation Aga Khan, a Swiss Corporate body registered under the Swiss Civil Code having their registered office at 32, Chemin Des Crets, Grand Saconnex, Geneva, Switzerland and also registered under the Companies Act 1956 (Act I of 1956) as a foreign company having amongst others their place of business in India at New Delhi by the hand of their constituted attorney Badruddin Ismail Merani residing at 15-C, "Shanax", 99, Lord Marg, Bombay 400 006, hereinafter called "the Purchasers" (which expression shall unless it be repugnant to the context or meaning thereof mean and include them and their successor or successors in title and their assigns) of the Other Part.

WHEREAS since the 11th day of July 1987, the Vendor has been seized and possessed inter alia of ALL THAT piece or parcel of land hereditaments and premises hereby conveyed and/or intended so to be and more particularly described in the Schedule hereunder written.

AND WHEREAS the Vendor has agreed to sell to the Purchasers and the Purchasers have agreed to purchase from the Vendor All the aforesaid land hereditaments and premises described in the Schedule hereunder written for the price of Rs. 1,80,000/-

AB-3

3

(Rupees one lac eighty thousand   ) and upon the
terms and conditions agreed to between them.

AND WHEREAS in pursuance of the aforesaid agreement,
the Vendor has agreed to execute these presents for vesting the
said land hereditaments and premises unto the Purchasers.

NOW THIS INDENTURE WITNESSETH that in pursuance
of the agreement aforesaid and in consideration of the sum of
Rs.1,80,000/- (Rupees one lac eighty thousand   )
to the Vendor paid by the Purchasers on or before the execution of
these presents (the payment and receipt whereof and that the same
is in full payment of the agreed price of the land hereditaments and
premises hereby conveyed, the Vendor doth hereby admit and
acknowledge and of and from the same doth hereby for ever
acquit, release and discharge the Purchasers) he the Vendor doth
hereby grant, sell, convey and assure unto the Purchasers forever
ALL the said land hereditaments and premises more particularly
described in the Schedule hereunder written (and all which said
land hereditaments and premises are hereinafter referred to for
brevity's sake as "The said premises") TOGETHER with all and
singular houses, outhouses, edifices, buildings, court-yards, areas,
compounds, sewers, ditches, fences, trees, drains, ways, paths,
passages, common-gullies, wells, waters, watercourses, plants,
lights, liberties, privileges, easements, profits, advantages, rights,
members and appurtenances whatsoever to the said premises or

AP-3

2

(Rupees one lac eighty thousand   ) and upon the terms and conditions agreed to between them.

AND WHEREAS in pursuance of the aforesaid agreement, the Vendor has agreed to execute these presents for vesting the said land hereditaments and premises unto the Purchasers.

NOW THIS INDENTURE WITNESSETH that in pursuance of the agreement aforesaid and in consideration of the sum of Rs.1,80,000/- (Rupees one lac eighty thousand   ) to the Vendor paid by the Purchasers on or before the execution of these presents (the payment and receipt whereof and that the same is in full payment of the agreed price of the land hereditaments and premises hereby conveyed, the Vendor doth hereby admit and acknowledge and of and from the same doth hereby for ever acquit, release and discharge the Purchasers) he the Vendor doth hereby grant, sell, convey and assure unto the Purchasers forever ALL the said land hereditaments and premises more particularly described in the Schedule hereunder written (and all which said land hereditaments and premises are hereinafter referred to for brevity's sake as "the said premises") TOGETHER with all and singular houses, outhouses, edifices, buildings, court-yards, areas, compounds, sewers, ditches, fences, trees, drains, ways, paths, passages, common-gullies, wells, waters, watercourses, plants, lights, liberties, privileges, easements, profits, advantages, rights, members and appurtenances whatsoever to the said premises or

CERTIFIED COPY

JOINT SUB-REGISTRAR-II
R.O. HYDERABAD   Scanned with OKEN Scanner

any part thereof belonging or in anywise appertaining to or with the same or any part thereof now or at any time heretofore usually held, used, occupied or enjoyed therewith or reputed or known as part or member thereof to belong or be appurtenant thereto AND also together with all the deeds, documents, writings, vouchers and other evidences of title relating to the said piece or parcel of land or ground hereditaments and premises or any part thereof AND ALL the estate, right, title, interest, use, inheritance, property, possession, benefit, claim and/or demand whatsoever at law and in equity of the Vendor in to out of or upon the said premises or any part thereof TO HAVE AND TO HOLD all and singular the said premises hereby granted, conveyed and assured or intended or expressed so to be with their and every of their rights, members and appurtenances unto and to the use and benefit of the PURCHASERS for ever subject to the payment of all rents, rates, taxes, assessments, dues and duties now chargeable upon the same or hereafter to become payable to the State Government or to the local Municipality or any other public body in respect thereof AND the Vendor doth hereby covenant with the Purchasers that notwithstanding any act, deed, matter or thing whatsoever by the Vendor or by any person or persons lawfully or equitably claiming by, from, through, under or in trust for him made, done, committed, omitted or knowingly or willingly suffered to the contrary he the Vendor now hath in himself good right, full power and absolute authority to grant, sell, convey and assure the said premises hereby granted, sold, conveyed and assured or intended or expressed so to be unto and to the use of the Purchasers in manner aforesaid AND THAT it shall be lawful for the Purchasers from time to time and at all times peaceably and quietly to hold, enter upon, have, possess and enjoy the said premises hereby granted and conveyed with their appurtenances and receive the rents, issues and profits thereof and of every part thereof to and for their own use and benefit without any suit, lawful eviction, interruption, claim and/or demand whatsoever from or by the Vendor or from or by any person or persons lawfully or equitably claiming or to claim by, from, under or in trust for him AND THAT free and clear and freely, clearly and absolutely acquitted, exonerated, released and forever discharged or otherwise by the Vendor well and sufficiently saved, defended, kept harmless and indemnified of, from and against all former and other estates, titles, charges and/or incumbrances whatever had made, executed, occasioned or suffered by the Vendor or by any other person or persons lawfully or equitably claiming or to claim, by, from, under or in trust for him or any of them AND FURTHER that the Vendor and all persons having or lawfully or equitably claiming any estate, right, title or interest at law or in equity in the said premises hereby granted and conveyed or any part thereof by, from, under or in trust for him the Vendor shall and will from time to time and at all times hereafter at the request and cost of the Purchasers do and execute or cause to be done

JOINT SUB-REGISTRAR-II
R.O. HYDERABAD

Scanned with OKEN Scanner

ထ္ဘ-၁

0

and executed all such further and other lawful and reasonable
acts, deeds, things, matters, conveyances and assurances in the
law whatsoever for the better, further and more perfectly and
absolutely granting, conveying and assuring the said premises and
every part thereof hereby granted and conveyed unto and to the
use of the Purchasers in manner aforesaid as shall or may be
reasonably required by the Purchasers, their successor or successors in title and their respective assigns or their or his counsel in
law.

IN WITNESS WHEREOF the Vendor by the hand of his
constituted attorney hath hereunto set and subscribed his name
the day and year first hereinabove written.

THE SCHEDULE ABOVE REFERRED TO

ALL the piece or parcel of land or ground of freehold
tenure subject to the provisions of land revenue laws with the
messuages tenement/tenements or dwelling house/houses standing
thereon situate lying and being on the West   side of
Chiragalli Lane   in the Village/Town/City of Hyderabad
              in the Tehsil/Taluka of Hyderabad West
District/Pargana Hyderabad   STATE of Andhra Pradesh
              and in the Registration Sub-district of Hyderabad
              and Registration District of Hyderabad
containing by admeasurement 2897.00 square metres (0100

.004 20:11 FROM : A R H C   91 40 9867<733   TO:90MHP:3811220   P. 5

№ D·3

square yards) or thereabouts and registered in the Books of the

Collector of Land Revenue under Old No.

New No.   Old Survey No.

New Survey No.   Cadastral Survey/City Survey

No.   of

Division and in the Books of the Local Municipality/Gram
                    Corporation
Panchayat of Municipal Ɫ · under Ward No. 5

and Street/House No. 5-9-498 to502 and bounded as follows:

That is to say: on or towards the East by Chiragalli Lane

                  on or towards the West by Super Bazaar

                  on or towards the North by Kuricabad Housing

Society Limited.,   and on or towards the South by Diamond Jubilee

School,   which property is shown sur- ~~
                                                      And
~~rounded by red coloured boundary lines on the Block Plan thereof~~
~~annexed hereto and marked "A".~~

SIGNED AND DELIVERED by   His Royal Highness
the withinnamed Vendor His Royal   Shah Karim Al-Huseini Aga Khan
Highness Shah Karim Al-Huseini   by the hand of his Constituted Attorney
Aga Khan by the hand of his con-
stituted attorney Ameerali Suleman
Rahimtoola in the presence of.

**CERTIFIED
COPY**

OFFICE OF THE
District Registrar   **JOINT SUB-REGISTRAR-II**
RED HILLS   R.O. HYDERABAD
HYDERABAD. T.S.

THE SEAL
OF THE
REGISTRAR
OF
HYDERABAD

APD-3

RECEIVED the day and year first hereinabove written of and from the Purchasers the sum of Rupees one lac eighty thousand being the full consideration money above mentioned to be by them paid to me.   } Rs. 1,80,000/-

WITNESS:

I SAY RECEIVED:

His Royal Highness
Shah Karim Al-Hussini Aga Khan
by the hand of his Constituted Attorney

Shri Amaarali Suleman to'double Constituted Attorney of His Royal Highness Shah Karim-Al-Hussini, Aga Khan Aga 47 residing at Orcee Fields, Flat No. 7 Maharshi Karve Road, Bombay 400 020 Executing party admits execution of the so called Deed of Conveyance.

Shri R. T. Camania Clerk of Messrs. Payen I Jamiaram and Madan Advocates and Solicitors, Bombay known to the Sub-Registrar stated that he knows the executants and identified them, his witness.

Date 30/3/1979

Sub-Registrar

Appendix 3

Pir Sadardin version of Harishchandra Story

The Holy Command has come from our Lord, Mowlana Hazar Imam. (Aga khan) This command must not be returned unfulfilled or ignored. Listen, O Brother and submit to this Divine Command from our Lord.

By obeying the Holy Command of our Lord, the Five Paandvas (*Five heroic brothers, central characters in the Indian epic, the Mahabharata).* attained an exalted position, their mother Maataa Kuntaa was also enlightened.

The Holy Command was also obeyed by Queen Taaraa Raani Lochanaa, who attained the exalted state by submission to it, and her husband, King Harishchandra and Prince Rohidaas, (their son) attained salvation as well.

Harishchandra declares to Taaraa Raani: "O my Queen, I have had a dream".

Here Pir Sadardeen begins to relate the incidence which led to King Harishchandra surrendering himself to the Divine Will. Queen Taara Raani used to go to the place of worship (Jamat Khana) late at night after her husband had gone to sleep. Eventually the King came to know about the queen's secret escapades. One day the King pretended to have gone to sleep while the Queen prepared to leave the palace.

The queen discarded her precious jewelry and adorned a simple garment. She then went to the stable and took their most beloved horse Hansloh and left for the place of worship (Jamat Khana). The King followed her discreetly as she left and observed the ceremonies she partook and was seen carrying a tray full of food offerings. The King is amazed at all the esoteric rituals and ceremonies that he had witnessed and upon her return, the King carefully questions her by implying a dream he had seen.

In the dream, I saw that you visited your parents' house, said Harishchandra.

O beloved and majestic King, I have no parents who I can visit said Taaraa Raani. She was an orphan.

The King took out a dagger, stood up in anger and said, "Queen, show me that tray!

The tray contained all the Juras (food offerings), that had been distributed at the congregational ceremonies.

The Queen turned to her Lord and invoked a prayer, O my Master, my Lord, you are the preserver of my honor and integrity.

Then (miraculously), the orange sweets, laddus and beejoraa (sweets), in the tray, turned to oranges, and the meat was transformed into red grapes.

The cooked grams turned into pearls, and the purees (flour fritters) turned into naagar (vine leaves).

After witnessing this miracle, the King put back the dagger and sits down, O Queen, show me this religious Path.

O beloved and majestic king, this Path is very difficult - it is like the edge of a sharp sword.

This path is very demanding, at first you must give your vital organs (heart & liver), and then you must also be prepared to give up the flesh of your body.

You will have to sacrifice your favorite horse Hansaloh, and also your (beloved) son, Rohidaas in charity.

You will also have to give up the luxury and privileges of your Kingdom of Ajodhaa, as well as the finery and jewelry worn by your beloved Queen Taara Raani.

The majestic king submitted to the Divine Will and sacrificed everything. He surrendered to God's Will i.e. became a Nizari.

Pir Sadardeen (composer of this Ginan) is imploring our Lord, Mowlana Hazar Imam - O our Lord, Master you are the grantor of salvation.

Appendix 4

Dua

Part 1

In the name of Allah, the most Beneficent, the most Merciful.

All praise is due to Allah, the Lord of the world, the most Beneficent, the most Merciful, the Lord of the Day of Judgment. Thee alone we worship and Thee alone we seek for help. Guide us to the right path, the path of those upon whom Thou hast bestowed favors, not of those cursed ones and nor of those who have gone astray.

I prostrate before Thee and I rely upon Thee; from the e is my strength and Thou art my protection, O Lord of the worlds.

(Sura Al Hamd)

O Allah, let Thy peace be on Muhammad – the Chosen, and on 'Aly – the favorite, and on the Imams –the pure, and on the evidence of Thy Authority – the Lord of the age and the time, our present living Imam, our Lord Shah Karim al-Husayni.

O Allah to Thee is my prostration and obedience.

Part 2

In the name of Allah, the most Beneficent, the most

Merciful.

"O ye, who believe, obey Allah and obey the Apostle and holders of authority from amongst you."

(Sura Nisa – Ayat 59)

"And We have vested (the knowledge and authority

of) everything in the manifest Imam."

(Sura Yaseen – Ayat 12)

O Allah, O our Lord, thou art the peace, and from
thee is the peace, and to Thee returneth the peace, O
our Lord, give us life of peace, and usher us in the
abode of peace. Blessed Thou art, our Lord, the
Highest, O the Lord of Majesty and Reverence.

O Allah, O our Lord, from Thee is my help and
upon Thee is my reliance; Thee alone we worship and
from Thee alone we seek support. O 'Aly, help me with
Thy kindness.

There is no deity except Allah, Muhammad is the
Messenger of Allah, 'Aly – the master of believers is
from Allah.
Our Lord Shah Karim al-Husayni is our present living in Imam.
O Allah to Thee is my prostration and obedience.

Part 3

In the name of Allah, the most Beneficent, the most
Merciful.

O Apostle, deliver (to the people), what has been revealed to thee from
thy Lord; and if thou did not do so, then thou hast not delivered His
Message, and Allah will protect thee from the people

(Sura Ma'eda –Ayat 67)

There is no deity except Allah, Ever-Living, the Eternal.

There is no deity except Allah, the Sovereign, the Ultimate Truth, the Evident

There is no deity except Allah, the Sovereign, the Ultimate Truth, the Certainty

There is no deity except Allah. the Lord of the Day of Judgment:

There is no hero except 'Aly. there is no sword except (his sword) 'Zulfiqar'.

Seek at the time of difficulties, the help of your Lord, the present living (Imam) Shah Karim al-Husayni.

O Allah to Thee is my prostration and obedience

Part 4

In the name of Allah, the most Beneficent, the most Merciful.

(O Prophet) Verily, those who give Thee their allegiance, they give it but to Allah (Himself); Allah's hand is upon their hands. Then he, who breaks it, he certainly breaks it against himself. And whoever fulfills what he has pledged with Allah. He shall in return reward him in plenty.

(Sura Fatah – Ayat 10)

O Allah, forgive us our sins, and give us our bread, and have mercy upon us, in the name of Thy closest Messengers and Thy holy Imams, and in the name of our Lord and our Imam, Shah Karim al-Husayni.

O Allah to Thee is my prostration and obedience.

Part 5

In the name of Allah, the most Beneficent, the most Merciful.

O ye who believe, do not betray Allah and the

Apostle and do not betray your trust while you know.

(Sura Anfal – Ayat 27)

O our Lord, forgive us our sins, and make our tasks

easy, and give us our bread, and have mercy upon us.

Thou art the Omnipotent.

O 'Aly, O Muhammad; O Muhammad. O 'Aly.

O Imam of the time, O our Lord, thou art my strength and Thou art my support and on Thee I rely.

O present O living, O Shah Karim al-Husayni, Thou art

the true manifest Imam.

O Allah to Thee is my prostration and obedience.

Part 6

In the name of Allah, the most Beneficent, the most Merciful.

Say: He is Allah, the One! Allah, the eternal Besought of all! He begetteth not nor was begotten. And there is none comparable unto Him.

(Sura-lkhlas)

O Allah, in the name of Muhammad – the chosen, and Aly – the favorite, and Fatima – the radiant, and (Hazrat) Hasan, and (Imam) Husayn.

O Allah in the name of our lord Aly

Our lord Husayn

Our lord Zainil 'Abideen

Our lord Muhammadinil Baqir

Our lord Ja'faris Sadiq

Our lord Ismail

Our lord Muhmmad bin Ismail

Our Lord Wafi Ahmed

Our lord Taqi Muhammad

Our lord Raziyiddeen Abdillah

Our lord Muhammadinil Mahdi

Our lord Qaim

Our lord Mansoor

Our lord Mu'izz

Our lord Aziz

Our lord Hakim bi Amrillah

Our lord Zahir,

Our lord Mustansiribillah

Our lord Nizar

Our lord Hadi

Our lord Muhtadi,

Our lord Qahir

Our lord 'Ala Zikrihis-Salaam

Our lord A'ala Muhammad

Our lord Jalaliddeen Hasan

Our lord 'Ala-iddeen Muhammad

Our lord Rukniddeen Khairi Shah

Our lord Shamsiddeen Muhammad

Our lord Qasim Shah

Our lord Islam Shah

Our lord Muhammad bin Islam Shah

Our lord Mustansiri-billah

Our lord Abdis-Salaam

Our lord Ghareeb Meerza

Our lord Abizzar Aly

Our lord Murad Meerza

Our lord Zulfiqar Aly

Our lord Nooridden Aly

Our lord Khalilillahi Aly

Our lord Nizar

Our lord Sayyid Aly

Our lord Hasan Aly

Our lord Qasim Aly

Our lord Abul Hasan Aly

Our lord Khalilillahi Aly

Our lord Shah Hasan Aly

Our lord Shah 'Aly Shah

Our lord Sultan Muhammad Shah.

And in the name of our lord and our present living Imam Shah Karim al-Husayni, have mercy upon us and forgive us (our sins).

Veri ly, Thou art the Omnipotent. And all the praise is

due to Allah, the Lord of the Worlds.

May you be blessed with the holy Deedar (glimpse) of our Lord.

O Allah to Thee is my prostration and obedience

Appendix 6

UK Council Authoritarianism

His Highness Prince Aga Khan Shia Imami Ismaili
Council for the United Kingdom

ANNOUNCEMENT BY THE NATIONAL COUNCIL

The National Council wishes to alert the Jamat regarding the activities of individuals and families that are contrary to a fundamental principle of the Ismaili Tariqah, of the absolute authority and prerogative of the Imam-of-the-Time.

The Jamat should remain aware that under the Ismaili Constitution, Mawlana Hazar Imam has established his Jamati institutions – around the world – to provide leadership to his Jamats, under his authority, guidance and direction. He has instituted a process for appointing Jamati leaders for a specified duration of time, and for communicating these appointments to the Jamat through his Talikas. Mawlana Hazar Imam has not appointed any leaders in any part of the world for the entirety of their lifetime, nor made leadership appointments that are intended to be of a hereditary nature.

We have received reports of some members of the Afghan Jamat who are misrepresenting themselves as Jamati leaders and agents, representatives, or "ministers" of Mawlana Hazar Imam and the Ismaili Imamat, with the intention of exerting authority over Jamati sections who are either persuaded or otherwise coerced into unauthorized religious activities that include making offerings purportedly for submission to the Imam-of-the-Time. These offerings are not being submitted to Mawlana Hazar Imam.

The Jamat of Afghanistan is integral to the Shia Imami Ismaili Tariqah of Islam, and there is no distinct or separate "Ismaili Tariqah of Afghanistan" – and Mawlana Hazar Imam is the sole *murshid* of all his *murids* throughout the world. In our Tariqah, as affirmed in the Ismaili Constitution, the Imams-of-the-Time has a direct relationship with each *murid*, and this relationship is not intermediated through any other individual or family.

The Jamat is respectfully reminded that Mawlana Hazar Imam has established formal Jamati channels for the purpose of submission of religious offerings, primarily through the Jamatkhanas and Mukhi-Kamadias around the world. Any individuals or families soliciting religious offerings or voluntary gifts, ostensibly on behalf of the Imam, are operating for their own purposes and these cannot be considered as legitimate religious offerings. These individuals are usurping the authority and prerogative of the Imam-of-the-Time.

Jamati members who choose to perpetrate or support these activities in any way should bear in mind that they may be subject to disciplinary action under provisions of the Ismaili Constitution.

Jamati members who have questions about the legitimacy of solicitations that they may be receiving are encouraged to approach the Mukhi-Kamadias and Mukhiani-Kamadianis who have been appointed to their positions by Mawlana Hazar Imam.

28.11.2024

Appendix 7

Agakhan Legal Exchange with Author

Direct line: [illegible]
[illegible]
[illegible]
Our Ref: [illegible]

29 October 2021

By Email: s_lalani@hotmail.com
Private and Confidential

Salim Lalani
113 Shinger Road
North Kellyville
NSW 2155
Australia

Carter-Ruck

Dear Sir

Our client: Ismaili Council for Australia and New Zealand

We have been consulted by our client in relation to the publication by you since 24 January 2021 of numerous video podcasts (in both English and Urdu) on YouTube and various other platforms under the title "Diary of a Common Man" (the "Videos").

There is an allegation repeatedly made in your Videos that His Highness the Aga Khan claims to be divine (the "Blasphemy Allegation"). This allegation is entirely false.

In reality, and as you know, in common with all Muslims, Ismaili Muslims affirm the fundamental Muslim testimony of truth, the Shahadah, that there is no God but Allah and that Muhammad is the first and final Messenger of God. The correct understanding of his role as Imam of the Ismaili Muslims is something His Highness has frequently made clear, for example in his address to both Houses of the Parliament of Canada in February 2014, in which he also clarifies the history of the role of the Imam in Shia interpretation of Islam and Imams in the Sunni interpretation of Islam.

As you also know, there have been numerous instances of extremist elements within some Muslim societies perpetrating intimidation and deadly violence against other Muslims, particularly Shia Muslims, around the world. Ismaili Muslims have been among those affected, and you are well aware both that large numbers of Ismaili Muslims live today in countries such as Pakistan and Afghanistan, where allegations of blasphemy can evoke strong and often violent sentiments and that Ismaili Muslims have historically been subject to violent and deadly attacks by such extremists.

You are on notice that the publication of the Videos (and particularly the Blasphemy Allegation) creates the risk of violence against Ismaili Muslims in those countries and also elsewhere.

That you are fully aware of this is readily evidenced in the Videos themselves where you mention the incident some five years ago in which 45 Ismailis were murdered on a bus in Pakistan and identify it as something for you to take into account in considering whether to publish Videos in Urdu. Nevertheless, you have chosen to proceed with publishing your Videos in Urdu.

We know that our client has sought to engage with you regarding this issue. Our client repeats its request to you to remove the Videos and to desist from posting further such videos as they are putting lives at risk. Should any harm come to Ismaili Muslims as a result of your Videos, you will bear responsibility for this.

Carter-Ruck Solicitors

6th Floor
Victoria House
London EC1N 8NN

+44 (0)20 7353 5005
DX 333 Chancery Lane
www.carter-ruck.com

PCR1-4383.2953

Yours faithfully

Carter-Ruck

Carter-Ruck

Oasis Counsel & Advisory

(Harcsh Jagtiani & Associates)

Udyog Bhavan, 1st Floor,
79 Walchand Hirachand Marg,
Ballard Estate, Mumbai - 400 001.
Phone : +91 22 6120 4600 / 4646
         +91 22 4913 4600 / 4646
Fax   : +91 22 6120 4647
         +91 22 4913 4647
E-mail : oasis@oasisadvisory.com

In association with :
D. M. HARISH & CO.,
Advocates
305-309, Neelkanth,
98 Marine Drive
Mumbai - 400 002.
Phone : (91-22) 2281 0517
Fax   : (91-22) 2281 9234
E-mail : dmharish@dmharishlaw.com

18th November 2021

To,
Carter Ruck Solicitors
The Bureau, 90 Fetter Lane
London EC1A 1EN

By email:- nigel.tait@carter-ruck.com
           Helena.shipman@carter-ruck.com
           james.watkins@carter-ruck.com

Re: Your notice dated 28th October 2021 to Mr. Salim Lalani (our
    client) on behalf of your client, the Ismaili Council for Australia and
    New Zealand

Dear Sir,

We have been instructed by our client, Salim Lalani, who is in receipt of your above captioned notice to deal with the same in the following manner:

1. Our client accepts that he has published videos under the title 'Diary of a Common Man' ("Videos") and stands by the contents thereof. The so called blasphemy allegation which your client claims "is entirely false" is denied by our client and he has ample proof to demonstrate that the Aga Khan indeed claims to be divine.

..2

Oasis Counsel & Advisory

-2-

2. In unnumbered paragraphs 3, 4 and 5, you have referred to the professed philosophy and religious beliefs of Ismaili Muslims as a community and the Shia and Sunni interpretation of Islam. Our client will not deal with those viewpoints as the same are not relevant for the purpose of this reply. However your client has touched upon some demographic aspects in certain parts of the world, particularly in Pakistan and Afghanistan, where according to your client the Videos and publications of our client "creates the risk of violence against Ismaili Muslims in those countries and also elsewhere". It is this aspect of your notice that our client refutes, for the purport of the Videos is only to highlight the claims to Godhood professed by the Aga Khan and to caution believers of Islam in general that such claims are being made for the purpose of attracting donations of huge sums of money ostensibly to be deployed for charitable and altruistic purposes. Our client has expressed grave and serious doubts as to the application of these funds and the means adopted by the Aga Khan in aggrandizing and accumulating these vast amounts. None of these facts and statements have been denied by the Aga Khan.

3. Your notice, by suggesting that our client's Videos would have the tendency to incite violence and therefore he should cease and desist from this publication, is unwarranted and unfounded. Our client sees no reason to remove the videos or to desist from posting any further Videos as they may, according to you, tend to put lives at risk in regions where the videos are viewed. The truth of the matter is that our client's comment on the Aga Khan's conduct and intentions are based on objective facts which are demonstrable and susceptible of proof and verification.

...3

Udyog Bhavan, 1st Floor, 29, Walchand Hirachand Marg, Ballard Estate, Mumbai - 400038. Phone+91 22 5829 4000 / 4646. Fax+91 22 6173 4667 Barwilliam@Oasisadvisory.com

Oasis Counsel & Advisory

-3-

4. It also surprises our client that though the theme and focus of his publication is the Aga Khan, no such refutation of the contents of the Videos is forthcoming from the Aga Khan himself but instead you have chosen to put our client to notice on behalf of another entity. Needless to say that our client will resist any attempt by your client at resorting to any legal process in a court of law as advised.

5. Without prejudice to what is stated above, and with a view to aim at amicably resolving the situation, our client suggests that an attempt at a conciliatory meeting be made between the Aga Khan or his representative and our client sometime in the near future. If this is acceptable to the Aga Khan, you may kindly convey the same to our client/ us to us, for and on behalf of our client.

Yours sincerely,

For Oasis Counsel & Advisory
Vandana Mehta Kumawat
Advocate

Appendix 8

Email To AKDN

Hello

We are an Australian based NGO researching His Highness the Aga khan and his humanitarian work.

Visiting AKDN website, we learnt that His Highness makes financial contribution towards humanitarian activities.

Would it be possible for AKDN to provide his historical contribution figures?

We are also intrigued to learn that donations from around the globe are invested rather than donated to the poor and marginalized.

As one of the most trusted and reputed networks of humanitarian agencies, we hope that AKDN will have no reservations engaging with us.

We thank you in anticipation.

Kind Regards

Salim Lalani
Director
Call To Wake Up Ltd

Call to
Wake Up